WELCOME TO
EARTH
AND OTHER PLAYS

WELCOME TO EARTH
AND OTHER PLAYS

The second collection of 30 five-minute
'remote theatre' plays created and performed
by Palestinian children

Edited by
Paul Dummett and Nick Bilbrough

GILGAMESH

Acknowledgement and thanks

I would like to acknowledge the support of Andy Hockley, Jan Patterson, Melissa Scott, Scott Thornbury and Tim Sayer [HUP board of trustees], all the judges of the competition, and UNRWA and the Palestinian Ministry of Education supervisors and teachers.

Huge thanks to all the Palestinian children who submitted plays for the competition. You are an enormous source of inspiration to us all!

Published by Gilgamesh Publishing 2019

Email: info@gilgameshpublishing.co.uk

www.gilgamesh-publishing.co.uk

ISBN 978-1-908531-86-5

© The Hands Up Project

Design by Eva Afifah

Cover Design by Mark Fenton

All rights are reserved. No part of this publication may be reproduced, stored in a retrieval system or transmitted in any form or by any means, electronic, mechanical, photographic or otherwise, without prior permission of the copyright holder

Contents

Foreword	9
Preface	11
Introduction	12

Chapter 1: The Right to Survival

A Stranger Within	22
Hope	28
The Story of a Homeland	32
Safsaf's Child	35
Welcome to Earth	40
The Ugly Ducklings	43

Chapter 2: The Right to Protection

Hands Up	50
I Can Smell Her	54
One World, Different Stories	58
The Living Song	62
The Shadow Girl	67
Don't Look Back	72
The Nightmare	77
Don't Kill the Olive	81
The Power of Words	84

Chapter 3: The Right to Participation

Hand in hand	9
I Can	9
It's Your Choice	10
Success Story	10
The Lord of the Show	10
The Sky's Your Limit	11
Tell Me Why	11
Who's the Master?	11

Chapter 4: The Right to Development

I Will Wait Until They Open the Gate	12
Othman the Honest	13
Future Gates	13
Don't Stop	13
Be What You Want	14
Ambition Play	14
The Play of the Play	15

• • •

This book is dedicated to Walter King for his ongoing support for the Hands Up Project.

The tree pictured on the cover is called Al Badawi and has been standing in what is now the village of Al Walajah (just outside Bethlehem) for around 5,000 years. It is widely believed to be the oldest olive tree in the world. In July 2019 15 children from Gaza, the actors in some of the plays featured here, were able to stand proudly beneath its branches and sing the Palestinian national anthem.

Foreword

By Benjamin Zephaniah

There was a time when I disliked theatre. The theatre buildings where I lived were inaccessible to people like me, and the people who visited them were not like me. But then my mother told me about the theatre she encountered in rural Jamaica. It was theatre created and performed by farmers, mothers, fathers, teachers, taxi-drivers and children. All written by them, about them, for them, and for anyone in the world who cared about them. I then went to Jamaica to experience this type of theatre for myself, and it turned me into a playwright.

As soon as I saw the work of the Hands Up Project, it took me right back. Not just back to Jamaica, but back to that feeling I had when I first encountered theatre that was relevant to myself, or the actual lives of the actors on stage.

The plays in this book are written by people who care, and with the use of modern technology. And with help by remote teachers who care, they are to be performed by young people who dare. They dare to put their bodies on the line and speak out, and they dare to express themselves and give it a go. They dare to reclaim theatre, and take it back to its roots.

Although this is a new way of producing plays for young people, its principles are closer to the original ideas of theatre than much of what you can see in the West End of London, or on Broadway in New York. I'm not saying that one form of theatre is better than another – all theatre has its place. I'm simply saying this theatre knows its place, regardless of how it's delivered.

This collection of plays, created and originally performed by young people in Palestine, can be used by teachers anywhere in the world. We know that these teachers do more than teach. They inspire. It's their creative fire and passion that becomes the inspiration that motivates the young people who will breathe life into these words. I am sure that given the right opportunities many of the young people who work with these plays could go on to greater things, but for now, it's great and inspiring that regardless of where they are, and the circumstances they are living under, they can start with this very great thing of making theatre.

Benjamin Zephaniah, August 2019

Preface

As an educational specialist working for UNRWA, I work closely with teachers and students. My main job is to support English teachers with their professional development, hoping that this will eventually be reflected in students' outcomes. Students in schools in Palestine live in a very vulnerable area which is highly unstable and subject to repeated conflict.

I feel so proud to be part of the Hands Up Project as I can see the impact of involving students in drama activities, remote theatre and see how the playwriting competition assists in the development of their language skills and their personal development as well.

Drama is an art, an outlet for self-expression and a very powerful way of learning. It provides an excellent platform for exploring different aspects of language, putting it into context and making it come to life. It engages and challenges students and keeps them actively involved. Drama provides psychosocial support for students. By playing different characters, students can express their feelings without being judged. This contributes to their overall well-being.

For two successive years, a group of Gazan kids have been given the chance to perform their winning plays outside Gaza. Gaza is a blockaded area, inconceivable as it probably is for most international readers of this book, travel in or out is, for them, a dream. Feedback from the kids states that it was a very rewarding, enriching and unforgettable experience. Many thanks to the Hands Up Project and I hope your work will reach more and more students in the coming years.

Rida Thabet, Education Specialist at UNRWA,
Palestinian Territories

Introduction

The first time I ever went to Gaza was in April 2017. Hands Up Project trustee, Scott Thornbury and I were due to speak at an UNRWA/British Council conference for Gazan teachers of English. Along with the 200 English teachers, there were also around 40 children there and one of the things that some of them did was to perform two plays in English that they had a created themselves. It was a lovely addition to the conference to have learner performances, but strangely it's something I rarely see at other training events for teachers around the world. It also gave me the idea for a competition. Scott and I discussed it on the long drive back to Jerusalem after the conference. The Hands Up Project playwriting competition was born!

Little did we know that we would end up receiving 88 entries for the competition from all over Palestine, and that we would publish 30 of them in a book 'Toothbrush and other plays' (Gilgamesh 2019) which we were proudly able to donate to all of the participating children and their teachers. The overall winners of the competition, the cast of *Inner Thoughts*, were invited to spend a week in the UK and they performed their play at the first Hands Up Project conference at Westminster University in April 2018, and also alongside Mark Thomas, the comedian, on stage at the Theatre Royal in Stratford, London. Not bad for five girls from Khan Younis who had never left the Gaza strip before and actually never even been in a theatre before!

In fact, the three plays that the judges ranked the highest (*Inner Thoughts*, *Window onto the Outside*, and *Live your Life*) were also invited to travel to the West Bank in November 2018 and they performed their plays on stage at Alrowwad Cultural Centre in Aida camp, Bethlehem and at the Freedom Theatre in Jenin. They also visited a Ministry of Education school in Bethlehem and performed their plays in front of the Deputy Minister of Education and the pupils and teachers of the school. This was a wonderful opportunity for the children who were performing, but also for the young people in the West Bank to meet young people from Gaza – a place which they are generally denied permission to travel to.

We have added subtitles to many of the plays so that they can be followed more easily by those who are not familiar with the Palestinian accent, and our Youtube playlist, 'Plays created by Palestinian children', has been seen by thousands of viewers around the world. The book 'Toothbrush and Other Plays' has been bought by teachers all over the world and learners of English in Peru, Russia, Spain, the UK and many other places are now reading the scripts, performing them and even sending the videos of their performances to the original authors in Palestine. As you can imagine, this is incredibly empowering for the children who originally made them.

Another thing that we never imagined happening was that many of these plays would be performed remotely through the online video conferencing tool, Zoom, by the original actors – both at schools through our regular lesson link ups and at conferences in Chile, Croatia, Turkey and the UK. All these successes gave us ideas for ways to improve the competition in 2018.

As a result, we launched the competition again at the end of 2018 with a number of changes to the rules. We kept the same system whereby there should be a maximum of 5 children acting, all aged 15 or younger and attending UNRWA or Ministry of Education Schools in Occupied Palestine. Again the play had to be a maximum of five minutes long and the students needed to submit both the script and a video recording of their performance. But whereas in the 2017 competition rules the film of the play could have been edited afterwards and sound effects or music added, this time we insisted that the plays should be filmed in one take only and that any special effects should be played in real time during the performance. We also made it a rule that the camera had to be kept completely still during the process of filming and that there could be no zooming in or out. There were three reasons for these changes.

Firstly, we wanted the experience of creating and performing a play to be as rich as possible in terms of language development; if the plays could be edited afterwards there was a danger that students could just repeat a line parrot fashion until they had said it as accurately as possible and then cut out all the parts with mistakes later. This may not provide a true reflection of the students' level of spoken English. If they only have one take the students have to practise the language much more intensively, and hold it in their heads for much longer, and this leads to greater internal processing of the language and ultimately more learning. The second reason for the changes was because we wanted the plays to be assessed less on the ability of the filmmaker to use the camera effectively (by zooming in on the actors' faces for instance during dramatic moments) and more on the abilities of the actors to get their messages across and move the audience through their skills in acting. Thirdly, we felt it was important that as many of the plays as possible could be later performed remotely through Zoom to international audiences around the world. When performing a play through Zoom there is no editing of course and there are no options for clever camerawork, so we wanted the competition to reflect this as far as possible. Of course, we also modified the assessment criteria to reflect these changes.

Fast forward a few months to a week before the submission deadline of 31st December 2018 and we were starting to wonder whether the changes to the rules had put people off as we had only received a handful of submissions. Had we made things too difficult at a time when everyone was focussed on the mid-semester exams? As it turned out, we should have been concerned for the opposite reason!

In fact, the vast majority of the plays arrived during the last two days before the deadline (many in the last few hours!), and we ended up receiving more than twice the number of entries of the previous year – a whopping 180 plays. We suddenly needed to find a much larger panel of judges than last year. We were lucky to be able to amass a team of 77 people in 23 different countries around the world; teachers of English, drama teachers, educational drama specialists, actors, storytellers, playwrights, directors, authors and university lecturers and students; people who write plays and act in them or direct them, but also people who just appreciate good theatre. There are too many comments and too many judges to include them all here but it is worth quoting some of the general comments from judges about the experience of watching the plays for the 2018 competition to give an impression of the impact the plays have had.

"Thanks again for letting me have the opportunity to look at another tranche of videos. As I'm sure you do, I get quite emotionally overcome watching these brilliant, talented young people and thinking of the danger and deprivation that they have to endure. Quite apart from anything else, I think these plays need to be shown to an international audience so people can see what it means to be a child in Palestine"

Ken Wilson, ELT author and drama specialist, UK

"That was difficult... so much talent, strong messages, deeply portrayed emotions, imaginative use of costume and scenery, well framed action, strong symbolism, sensitive use of music, passion and belief, taking on and tackling 'big issues', expressing mature themes with feelings. It's quite overwhelming to see young people looking at such deep issues and finding ways of expressing them with heart and soul. Power to you all! Thank you for opening many windows in my life..."

Michael Loader, professional storyteller and actor, UK

"Once again thank you for asking me to watch these short plays, and for reminding me how powerful drama and telling stories in different ways can be. It was wonderful to see such a range, and I can't wait to show them to my own students, and to do this kind of thing where I work. What a stunning level of English these young people have!"

Sophie Roberts, ESOL and drama teacher, UK

"Thanks very much for inviting us to take part in judging these very powerful plays. A real privilege – we were very moved. Please tell all the young actors and their teachers how much we enjoyed seeing them down here on the other side of the world!"

Jill and Charles Hadfield, ELT materials writers, New Zealand

"I'm so glad to see so many talented young children and also happy to know that they had the opportunity to learn through making a play, to reflect upon their own reality, to interact with each other and through the camera, to use their creativity and imagination. Congratulations to you all!!!"

Caroline Aragão, English teacher and actress, Brazil

"Thank you to all the young people for the immense privilege of watching and judging their plays. One criteria for assessing theatre is does the play help us understand the experience of being human. Well together they all do this, tremendously"

David Mowat, musician and theatre director, UK

Eventually the judges whittled down the 180 plays to 18 finalists, proportionally represented by plays from the West Bank, from Gaza, made by boys and girls, and by younger and older children. All of these plays are being invited to perform at theatres in the West Bank at some point in 2019.

One overall winner was chosen from the finalists, *'I can smell her'* and the four winning 10 and 11 year old girls from Gaza Elementary B school were invited with their teacher to spend a week in the UK in April 2019 to perform at the Hands Up Project conference at the University of Central Lancashire in Preston.

Here are the 18 finalists' plays, listed in alphabetical order.

A Stranger Within – Al Rimal Prep Girls School A

Don't Look Back – New Khan Younis Prep Girls School

Hand in Hand – Abasan Prep Girls School

Hands Up – Al Aqsa Elementary School B

Hope – Hajjah Girls Secondary School, Qalqilia

I Can – Mae'n prep boys school

I Can Smell Her – Gaza Elementary Girls 'B' School

It's Your Choice – Beach Prep Girls School C

I Will Wait Until They Open The Gate – Beach Elem. Co-ed School (C)

One World Different Stories – Al Rimal Prep Girls School B

Othman the Honest – Khan Younis prep boys school

Success Story – Japanese Girls School, Aqqaba

The Living Song – Beit Hanoun Elm. Co-ed "D" School

The Lord of Show – Tel al-Sultan Elementary school

The Play of the Play – Al Fukhari Prep. Girls School

The Shadow Girl – Asma Prep Girls B School

The Sky is your Limit – Al Madina Al Monawara Prep Girls

The Story of a Homeland – Al Madina Al Munawara Girls School, Rafah

These 18 finalists are included here, as well as twelve other plays. Last year the plays were organised into four thematic chapters: *Family, School, Freedom and Imagination*. This year we have arranged them according to the United Nations' four fundamental rights of the child: the right to survival; the right to protection; the right to participation; and the right to development. It was extremely difficult to decide which plays should be included and while this framework made it easier for us, it meant that some excellent plays haven't been included because they didn't fit well into these four categories.

I would, however, like to personally offer my sincere congratulations to every single student, teacher and school in Palestine who took part in the competition by submitting a play. You are all winners! Together you have told your stories of what it is to be a young person in Palestine – first, to the judges, and now these stories are being told again to many, many more people around the world via our Youtube channel.

And congratulations to all participants too for throwing yourselves into what I believe is the first *Remote Theatre* competition to take place anywhere in the world. Doing the competition as remote theatre (one take only with a fixed camera position, and no editing) has levelled the playing field a little bit, because it means that the actors have to depend much more on their abilities to use English and on their acting skills, rather than on the techniques of the film maker. It's more challenging, but better for English language development, and I'm so pleased to see that you've risen to this challenge so well - with creativity, commitment and sheer hard work.

A final, but significant reason for doing the competition in this way is so that the learners who conceived the plays have ready-made remote theatre pieces which can be performed through Zoom at schools, or in theatres, or at conferences around the world. And we will do everything we can to enable this to happen as much as possible. When these plays are performed with clarity and from the heart, and are done in a way that helps us to see that it could be us in your story, then what may happen is that *your* story becomes *our* story. And this really is what our work in the Hands Up Project is all about.

Nick Bilbrough, Hands Up Project founder,
August 2019

Chapter 1
The Right to Survival

A child's right to survival encompasses their right to be born, to have access to a minimum standard of nutrition, shelter and clothing, and the right to live their lives with dignity. The plays in this section highlight the fragility of these most fundamental rights for many Palestinian children. In **A Stranger Within** and **The Story of a Homeland,** we hear the poignant voices of the displaced and dispossessed. **Safsaf's Child** dramatizes an incident during the Nakba (the eviction from their homes of half the Palestinian population in 1948) where a crying child endangers the fleeing refugees, while **Hope** gives us a stark view of what life is like under occupation. The plays **Welcome to Earth** and **The Ugly Ducklings** each view life in Palestine from an original perspective: the former from the point of view of aliens and the latter through the eyes of imaginary, fairy-tale characters.

A Stranger Within

'A Stranger within' was created and performed by Judy Eid, Farah Thabet, Lana Al Ajez, Aya Zahran and Lana Abu Zbeida from Al Rimal Prep A UNRWA school, Gaza, with support from their teacher, Fatma Aljarrah. A recording of the play, performed by the actors is available here...

bit.ly/astrangerwithin

What the judges said: "A beautifully written play delivered in rhyming lines with passion and conviction. A powerful message about our indomitable human spirit."

Judy: How hard it is to live in a land

Where no longer you feel safe

Or have no food in hand

I start questioning what home really means

A blue sky? Birds fly?

Or hills that are green?

(Pictures of the different things mentioned may be shown behind)

A stranger within, I stand broken

No home that really feels like home

No home where you find wars, famine and broken children

(more pictures may be shown of a bomb blast, a Yemeni girl who has died from starvation, an orphaned child)

Thus, I made a decision

To move to another land

To expand my vision

In a suitcase, a few things I put inside

My identity and the certificate of my origin

(she put some papers inside a suitcase and picks it up. She looks all around her, appearing to be lost)

I dragged my heavy legs and walked away

Suddenly a voice is heard from far far away

Navy Soldier: You're forbidden! You're not leaving

Judy: There is no way, there is no way!

　　　　I did not listen

　　　　I rushed to the borders

　　　　I was blocked! I was pushed away

　　　　They said:

Soldiers: These are orders

　　　　Go back! You have no right to pass

Judy: I screamed: no no! This is unfair!

　　　　I'll find a way and with the world I'll share

　　　　The agony and suffering we Palestinians pay

　　　　I'll find a way! I'll find a way

　　　　I ran to the sea, forth and back

　　　　It was rough! The clouds were black

　　　　It was scary

　　　　But I rode in a ferry

　　　　Only three miles I crossed

　　　　but eventually by the soldiers I'm pushed

　　　　With guns and pistols they shouted.

Soldiers: *[preventing her from going forward]*

　　　　Go back! You have no right to pass

Judy: I screamed while on the shore

This is unfair, this is unfair

I'll find a way and with the world I'll share

The agony and suffering we Palestinians pay

I'll find a way! I'll find a way

I tried the land. I tried the sea but I failed

It's time to try the air

But no way, for we are in a prison

Everything is tightly closing

Nothing is permitted to fly over

Only drones and warplanes that can hover

This is unfair! This is unfair

[pictures of warplanes may be shown]

With a broken heart, I sat alone

So sad with lots of pain running in my bones

With tears falling all over my face

Suddenly a kiss from the sun fell on my cheeks!

Quickly I looked and wiped my tears

A soft voice called my name

The sun: Don't cry or feel the pain

One day, you'll be free

Just have faith

The same sun that shines on free nations

will shine your way one day

Nothing remains the same forever

The tyrant will one day fall

And free the nation will be all

Have faith my little angel, have faith

Judy: I wiped my tears away

Held my little hands together and started to pray:

Oh, Lord

Salvation and peace I ask you

Salvation and peace I ask you

[She sits on the ground, crying. The sun comes from behind her and puts her soft hands on Judy's cheeks. Judy wipes her tears away, holds her hands together and prays to God.]

***

Fatma says...

Palestinian children are very creative and talented. They just wait for the chance to be discovered and for their voices to be heard. Once they sense that there is an opening for that opportunity, they seize it and amaze everyone.

My students sensed that chance in the Hands Up project's play writing competition. They had an idea in mind and they wanted to pass it on to the whole world. And what better way than drama to communicate themselves?!

„A Stranger Within" was the name of the play my children made. Through that play, and since they live in the largest open air prison in the world, they wanted to tell the whole world about the struggle and suffering they live in; about the obstacles they face whenever they want to move or travel for purposes such as medication or education. They feel like that they are trapped and there is no way out. However, hope is never lost for the adamant Gazans. They believe that one day their dreams will come true and salvation and peace will be achieved.

True that the making of the play needed lots of planning. But with the minimum resources it was filmed and finally made.

First, I had a meeting with the girls who showed their greatest desire and abilities to participate in the competition. We agreed on the topic we wanted to communicate and then the students met to write the script. After that, they sought my help with editing and enhancing the language. Together, we achieved the final version of the script to be acted. With a fixed camera and a very simple scene inside one of the rooms at our school, we filmed the play and submitted it to the organizing committee of the competition. Thankfully, we were among the 18 finalist plays.

The play was literally the lungs" for those young stifled girls to breathe the fresh air beyond the besieged Gaza strip. This experience enriched the students at many levels. First, their thinking skills grew stronger and stronger. They started thinking of extremely creative ways to tell the world their message. Secondly, teamwork and collaboration were achieved in every step of the making of the play. Students managed to work within a team, leaving their selfish desires behind. They re-discovered their hidden talents in acting and they worked really hard to enhance them all the way to the end. Thirdly, their language improved greatly, both the segmentals and suprasegmentals. They learned how to control the pitch of their voices and how to use their facial expressions and body language. Adding to all those wonderful benefits the children got out of this experience, the play was their only way to break the siege and travel to the other part of their stolen land: the West Bank, specifically Jerusalem. Emotionally, their hearts leapt from their chests. They felt that finally we are here; we are in the play that we were forever longing for. In other words, their characters have changed greatly and their dreams came true and it is all because of this great experience.

Hope

'Hope' was created and performed by Farah Issam Hamad, Leena Bajes Batta, Sarah Barakat Hamad, Thekra Mohamad Khlaif and Tuqa Mamoon Ghanem from Hajjah Girls Secondary School, Qalqilia, Palestine with support from their teacher, Nasra Juma Qaddomi. A recording of the play, performed by the actors is available here...

bit.ly/HopeHGSS

What the judges said: "Heart-felt performance showing a snapshot of daily life under occupation. Overcomes the challenges of filming outside really well."

Characters: Father, **Abu Ahmad;** *his wife,* **Amal;** *his daughter,* **Farah;** *his son,* **Ahmad** *and* **Israeli soldiers**.

Mum: Three months! The last time, I've been arrested for three months. They deprived me of my family. They tortured and mistreated me. They used force and were violent with me. They dragged me out of my house in the middle of the night. My kids were shouting and crying. They arrested me for no reason like sixteen thousand Palestinian women who have been arrested since 1967 at different periods. And of those 63 are still in prison, and among them there are 21 mothers and 7 girls under 18. But I have hope.

Father: Come on, my son, dig and watch out for the roots of the trees. The olive tree is like your mother; you should always take care of it and protect it from any harm.

Son: Dad, look! The soldiers are coming.

Soldier: Hey, what are you doing here kid?

Son: What are we doing?! Don't you see that we are digging our land, planting and taking care of our olive trees?

Soldier: Your land! Ha ha ha!!! Soon it's going to be ours. We will take it from you by force and there will be no olive trees. We'll cut them all.

Farah: But olive trees are the source of life for us as Palestinians. They provide us with olive oil which is our golden symbol. Allah mentioned it in the Holy Qur'an, so it's a holy tree. Dad even thinks the olive trees are as precious as his sons and daughters.

Father: Listen, soldier, we are the rightful owners of this land. Its soil is mingled with our sweat. We cultivate it and take care of it. So you have no right to take it.

Soldier: Get out, stupid fool. Your wife is inciting the women against the Israelis while you are planting. This land is close to the settlement, so you are not allowed to enter, plough, plant or step inside it. It will be confiscated for security reasons.

Son: How dare you? This land is ours and you are the intruders. You should get out. We are fed up with your vicious actions against us as children. We don't live a normal life like other children in the world. You are the last occupation in this world and your time will end soon.

Soldier: Don't talk to me like that. Step back, you idiot. *[Pushes the son back]*

Father: Don't shout at my son and don't touch him. This is our land, villain. I don't know where you come from – America, Britain, Russia or wherever. You are the intruders. If you think you can break us by destroying our trees and houses or murdering our innocent men, women and children you are deluded. We are the original owners of this land. You don't appreciate international laws, human rights or resolutions which give us the right to live freely and independently like any other nation. You've affected each and every home in Palestine. We all suffer from your brutality and violence. It's enough! Enough! Enough!

[The soldiers attack. They start shooting so one shot hits the father in his chest and he starts bleeding. They also arrest the son, cuff his hands and take him to an unknown place]

[The daughter starts crying and shouting]

Farah: Where are you dad? Wake up don't leave me!!! Dear brother! Why are you taking him? Why are you doing this? He's just a little boy. He has done nothing. You arrested my mum. Wasn't it enough?! You took our happiness and freedom.

We Palestinians love our land and we will never give it up even if we die for it. We believe that one day we will be free. And Allah will help us.

We will never lose hope!

We will never lose hope!

Hope! Hope! Hope!

***

Nasra says...

First of all, our present situation and the suffering that we feel due to the violent measures placed on us as Palestinians living under the Israeli occupation played an important role in making this play. The topic that we tackled is of great importance and through it we hoped to send a message to the whole world, stating that the acts of confiscating land and depriving Palestinians the right to reach and cultivate their land should be put to an end. It's against all human rights to ask us as the legal owners of the land to have permits to reach our land and cultivate it. The topic of the play was suggested by the girls who acted in it and they wrote it after we had discussed the topic and agreed on the characters involved. The script was first written by the students and I then checked it to make the final copy. My students benefitted a lot from making and acting the play. First of all, it was a chance for them to express themselves and practise the English language in acting. It was also an opportunity for others to be encouraged to participate in similar future activities, as this was the second time that we have participated and reached the finals in this competition. Finally, the experience was something vital to build upon for encouraging the students to improve their English language skills through acted out situations; this helps them to have self-confidence and fluency in spoken as well as written English. Thanks for your encouragement and appreciation

The Story of a Homeland

'The Story of a Homeland' was created and performed by Tala Mohammed Hafiz Abu Abdu, Jana Raafat Radwan, Dana Mohammed Hafiz Abu Abdu, Nour Al Huda Sameer Abu Sultan and Farah Anwar Al Shaer from Al Madina Al Munawara Girls School, Rafah, Gaza with support from their teacher, Soha Abdulmajeed Isleem. A recording of the play, performed by the actors is available here ...

bit.ly/storyofahomeland

> *What the judges said: "A creatively planned shadow theatre performance that tells the story of Palestine. Ingenious and fine physical acting."*

Narrator:

Once upon a time there was a happy couple.

They lived happily and after few months they received a beautiful baby boy.

The child grew day by day in front of their eyes.

He went to school every day.

The family lived in peace.

Suddenly some people occupied their land and expelled them.

Risking all they rode the sea.

They reached a new modern country.

They lived there and the boy sold newspapers to help his family.

He completed his studies in medicine.

This is the day of his graduation.

Scene: graduation day

Boy:

Praise and thanks to Allah who grants me success and excellence. I'm standing here today to deliver my graduation speech ... so thanks Allah again. I dedicate my success to my parents and to my country, Palestine; Palestine, the sad and wounded; Palestine, my homeland from which my family and I were expelled. But we will return one day, I promise. I will help ill people there, inSha'allah.

Soha says...

The five little students were all from the primary stages: Tala is 11 years old, Jana, Dana, Farah and Nour are all 9 years old. Our play had a new and creative idea: a shadow play. Everything was challenging. It was difficult to prepare a place to practise performing the play.

We used a white piece of cloth as the screen and an overhead projector to help shifting the scenes. Moreover, we used music to let us live the story truly. Furthermore, it wasn't easy to perform different characters, animals, trees and things because of the age and limited number of the participants. But by practising every day and creating a very nice atmosphere for these kids, they succeeded in performing it creatively.

My students benefited a lot from this experience. They learnt how to work co-operatively, how to respect each other, how to use their bodies smoothly to create different shapes, and finally to use the English language fluently in writing and performing the play.

It was an interesting experience. Thanks, Hands Up Project!

Safsaf's child

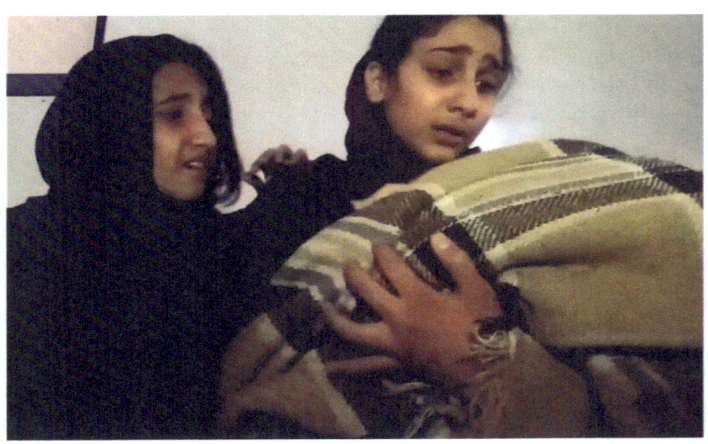

Safsaf's Child was created and performed by Malak, Leen, Loura and Hala from Qabatia secondary Girl's school, Occupied Palestine with support from their teacher, Salam Nazzal. A recording of the play, performed by the actors is available here ...

bit.ly/safsafschild

What the judges said: "A dramatic and imaginative recreation of a real event from the Nakba of 1948. Very moving close-up camera work."

Scene: The play opens with a frozen image of the old man, old woman and the mother carrying her child of one year and ten months who are all terrified.

Narrator: In a very small village called Safsaf on a very dark night, there was a group of terrified Palestinian refugees escaping from the war in 1948 to the Lebanese borders. It was an ethnic cleansing of this village. The group consisted of the old man who was the leader, old woman, mother and her child of one year and ten months. A terrifying incident happened to this group while escaping. Let's see what it was.

Old man: *[very terrified and angry]* Quickly! We must leave this place. They may see us. Quickly! The soldiers will see us and know where we are now. [shouting] Shut him up. *[The child is crying]*

Mother: *[very scared of the old man]* OK, OK. No, my baby, no.

[The sound of a bomb dropping]

Old man: *[putting his hand on his head]* Oh, my God. What is there? How can we leave now?

Old woman: Listen! Listen! The situation is getting worse.

[The child continues crying]

Old man: *[angry]* Still crying?! I told you, shut him up. Shut him up!

Old woman: *[gives the mother a loaf of bread she has hidden in her dress]* Don't worry, don't worry. He is surely hungry. Take this, take this.

Old man: Give it to him. Give it to him.

Mother: Oh, Thank you. Yes, he is surely. *[She divides the loaf into two halves, gives one to the child, the other to the old woman]*

[The child is quiet now]

 Old man: Look! I'm going to see if there is safety in this road. Stop here. Don't move a step.

[The child starts crying]

Mother: Oh, my God. Help me. Help me.

Old woman: Why is he still crying?

Mother: *[Trembling]* I think, he needs the entire loaf.

Old woman: *[takes a needle and thread from her dress and sews the two halves back together]* OK, OK, never mind. I will sew it now, although it's very dark.

Mother: *[Afraid of the old man's anger]* I will help you. I will help you.

[For a moment the child is quiet]

Mother: Alhamdulillah, he is quiet now.

Old woman: Alhamdulillah, Alhamdulillah. Our leader is late, isn't he?

[Again the child is crying]

Mother: Oh, my baby. Calm down, calm down.

Old woman: Shhhh. Why is he crying again?

Mother: *[Crying]* The stitches started to come undone. He needs the entire loaf. How can I get one?

Old man: *[returns and he is angry]* I saw many youths have been killed there. Oooh, still crying? *[comes over the child]* Take it, take it.

Mother: He doesn't want it.

Old man: *[shouting]* Then, kill him.

Mother: Ohhhhh!

Old man: They may hear his voice, see us and come.

Mother: Oh my god. No! Noooooo!

Old woman: No. No. Calm down my baby, calm down.

Old man: *[Threatening]* Look! I saw a well over there. Give him to me. I will throw him in it.

Mother: No. No. I will wrap him with this heavy blanket. His voice will become lower.

Old man: See ! Many youths have been killed there. Which is better to be killed: this child or those youths?! And because of him they may find us and kill us. *[shouting]* He must die.

[Another bomb drops]

All: *[putting their hands on their heads]* Ooooh!

Old man: What is there? I can see a group of people escaping. Oooh! Others are shouting. *[talking to the old woman]* Look! Did you see?

Old woman: Yes, yes.

Old man: Oooh! I told you. Shut him up!!

Mother: *[completely terrified]* I'm doing that. Be quiet my baby, pleeeease.

Old woman: Let's leave this place.

Old man: Yes, we must find a safer one. [pointing with his stick] Go ahead, go ahead. *[They leave the place and head to the Lebanese border. The old man is behind them supporting the child's head on his mother shoulder trying to silence him]*

Old man: *[breathing heavily]* Finally, we've got to the border. I want to take a rest.

Old woman: I want to too. I'm very tired.

Mother: *[looking at her child]* Baby. Oh, baby, baby! What's up with him?!

[Old man leaves the stage]

Mother: *[showing her child to the old woman]* Is he dead?! Is he dead? Oh, my Baby!! *[Old woman tries to calm her down]*

Mother: *[Raising her child to us says]* You died! Who is responsible for your death?! Who? You? You? Or you? Who killed you my child?! Whooo?

***

Salam says...

The play Safsaf's Child was mainly suggested by my students with the help from their history teacher. They wanted to show the world how this village, like hundreds of other villages was damaged , and how this child, as thousands of other children also, was killed .The play is based on a real story which happened in Safsaf village in 1948. It is mentioned by the Lebanese writer, Elias Khoury, in his novel called 'The Gate of The Sun'. With regard to the loaf of bread, my students said that it is considered as a protection collar for the group. Because the old woman and the mother were afraid of the old man's anger, they sewed the two halves back together to silence the child. But, the loaf of bread did not succeed in protecting the child from death. Here is the question: who killed Safsaf's Child? The old man who was afraid of the Israeli soldiers? The mother who was afraid of the old man's anger? Or the Israeli soldiers? Aren't the Israeli soldiers the main reason for killing the child?

We all consider that participating in this competition has been the greatest experience in our lives. It was a very interesting challenge for all of us. After we had finished acting, we became like a family, especially because I hadn't known these students before.

Welcome to Earth

'Welcome to Earth' was created and performed by Mahmoud Kafafi, Rida Amouri, Ahmed Afghani, Abdul-Rahman Madi, Ahmed Abboush from Askar Boys UNRWA school, Nablus, Palestine with the support of their teacher Ghada Hamdan. A recording of the play, performed by the actors is available here ...

bit.ly/welcometoearth

What the judges said: "A view of the world from the perspective of aliens arriving from another planet. Original, simple and effective."

[Sound of a space vehicle as five aliens from space land on Earth]

Taro: Ohhh..we've landed safely !

All Aliens: Hey..! Hey!!! *[They hug each other]* Earth.. Earth the beautiful blue planet!!!

Fin: And ..now, let's see ..What should we do?

Bell: We should try to find somewhere to live!

Nan: But where?

Wim: Mmm... I think we should look for a good, safe place, my friends. Let's go and look in different places, then meet back here. Everyone can tell us where they went.

All: OK, Wim, OK. You're right. *[They give each other a hi-five then fly away]*

[Soon they appear again, milling about in front of the camera]

[Finally, they meet back together, looking sad, surprised, most of them disappointed with humans' wrongdoings on Earth]

Taro: There are many wars on Earth. Humans kill each other. They use bad weapons. These weapons kill many children! How could this happen on Earth?!

Fin: I've seen many poor people .. homeless .. looking for food. No one looks at them. There is so much food on Earth, but many people are still hungry!

Bell: Well, I was in a big city. There were many cars. They smell of very bad gas. So much pollution on Earth.

Nan: I don't think humans on Earth are so bad. I'm lucky!! I've seen nice, good people. Farmers grow crops. Teachers teach children at school. Doctors help sick people...

All: *[smiling]* Ohhhh!

Wim: Well, the weather on Earth is getting worse because of humans' activities. They cut down so many trees. Earth is getting hotter and its ice is melting!

All: Ohhhhh, this is so bad ... so dangerous for life on Earth.

Wim: So what should we do, my friends? Shall we stay ... or look for life on another planet?

[They stand in a circle, look at each other and raise their hands]

All: Earth is beautiful. We will stay here and make it a better place!

The End (or is it just the Beginning?)

***

Ghada says...

I wanted our students to enjoy drama as an art, to experience acting and the way it can stretch the imagination and build confidence. I wanted them to experiment with drama as a tool for learning English by using it in different contexts, both imaginative and real situations.

Through his work in Palestine as a teacher trainer, Mr. Nick Bilbrough conducted quality training at UNRWA schools. His drama training ignited a good interest in drama among teachers and encouraged them to integrate it even more in teaching English and in encouraging their students to create their own plays.

As a teacher, I have always tried to explore students' interests and this topic particularly appealed to their imaginations. The play is written using simple language, but it addresses global themes.

The students were a little shy at first because it was their first experience of acting. However, they tried it and enjoyed their roles and use of English. I also noticed that they became closer friends. They told me that in high school they'd like to try acting.

The ugly ducklings

'The Ugly Ducklings' was created and performed by Dana Meqdad, Jana Hijjo, Maryya Hammad, Raghad Sammour and Rewaa Abu-jahjouh from Beach Elementary Co-ed C School, an UNRWA school in Gaza, Palestine, with the support of their teacher, Mervat M. Abdelnabi. A recording of the play, performed by the actors is available here ...

bit.ly/theuglyducklings

What the judges said: "An engaging story mixing fairy tale characters with the real-life reality of life in Gaza. Powerfully acted and ultimately uplifting."

Scene One: *Three Palestinian girls are playing. Suddenly, there is the sound of an explosion.*

Girls: *[shouting]* Oh No! Mummy! What happened? I'm afraid!

[Cinderella and Laila appear suddenly]

Scene Two

Laila: What's going on?

Cinderella: It's a terrifying place.

[Laila & Cinderella walk toward the 3 girls]

The hope of Gaza: Who are you?

Laila: *[terrified]* I'm Laila and this is my friend Cinderella. We come from legend world.

Cinderella: Who are you?

The hope of Gaza: I'm the hope of Gaza.

The wishes of return: I'm the wishes of return.

The peace of Jerusalem: I'm the peace of Jerusalem.

[Sad Music]

The hope of Gaza: *[Crying]:* Why did you leave books and come here for wars and destruction?

Cinderella: *[sadly]* We came to listen to your stories.

The wishes of return: *[crying]* Our stories are similar: poverty, death, siege, wars everywhere.

The peace of Jerusalem: *[angrily]* I advise you to leave our country, Palestine. We aren't like the other children. We are the Ugly Ducklings.

Laila: *[sadly]* Oh my God. You don't live in peace?

The hope of Gaza: *[sadly]* Peace! Peace! We dream of living in peace! But peace... justice ... equality are just words we heard from our ancestors.

Scene Three

[Peaceful Music]

The wishes of return: I hope to be an artist and paint the sky with my favourite colours. To draw a smile on my father's face.

The hope of Gaza: I hope to be an actress. On the stage, I want to shout! I want to shout! And hear the audience clapping...

[The fans of Hope start clapping]

The hope of Gaza: ...and calling my name: Hope! Hope! Hope!

[The fans of Hope start screaming and calling her name)

The hope of Gaza: *[sadly]*: But I need a witch to help me like your witch, Cinderella!

Scene Four

The peace of Jerusalem: I hope just to live in peace.

[The sound of an explosion]

The peace of Jerusalem: *[angrily]* I hate wars. I hate the sound of explosions. I hate it!

[The peace of Jerusalem starts crying]

Laila: Oh dears, your dreams will not be lost. Peace needs Education!

Cinderella: Laila is right!

[Cinderella starts to encourage the three girls]

Cinderella: I suffered a lot until my prince came. Your prince is education. Let's shout to the whole world:

All the girls: *[Together]* It's our right to learn.. to play.. to live in peace.

Scene Five

Laila: Let's sing this song! A song of peace!

[Music of the song of Peace. The girls sing together]

If I could write a magic song

That everyone could sing,

I would write of love

Of hope and joy

And things that peace could bring...etc.

Laila: Do you like the song?

The girls: Yes! It's good!

[Laila & Cinderella want to return to their fairy tales]

Laila & Cinderella: Now... Good Bye!

The three girls: No! Don't go!

Cinderella: We promise to return when you return to your land.

Everyone: Good bye!

[Laila & Cinderella go back to their fairy tales, and the girls go home]

***

The ugly ducklings

Mervat says...

This play was inspired by the fairy tales that Palestinian students love, which connect fairy tales with the reality of the actual situation in Palestine. In our school, we have an annual project called "Act, Sing and play". This was one of the plays that the students wrote, and was revised and developed with the help of Mrs. Mervat Abdel-Nabi, their English teacher, and the leader of the project. Our participation in the Hands Up Project was encouraged and supervised by the school principal, Mrs. Ghada Karawan.

The benefits of the play were very obvious in the physical, emotional and social sides of the students' characters. They became more self-confident, and started to think outside of the box. They also became more confident going into unfamiliar situations and in problem solving, critical and creative thinking. They started to trust their ideas and abilities. They also developed their values of citizenship, imagination, cooperation, concentration, communication skills, and their memory. Finally, the students' appreciation for Arts and Culture increased significantly because that experience brought joy and fun into their daily life at school.

Chapter 2
The Right to Protection

The Right to Protection enshrines the child's right to be protected from danger, from neglect, from all types of exploitation and from abuse, whether at home or outside the home. Many of the plays in this chapter look at family relationships: the importance of family in **The Living Song**; the loss of a loved one in **Don't Look Back** and **I Can Smell Her**; the effect of modern social media addiction on family in **Don't Kill the Olive** and **The Shadow Girl**; and the fragility of young aspirations in **The Power of Words** and **The Nightmare**. Others, like **One World, Different Stories** and **Hands Up** deal with the wider needs of all humans to connect, to understand each other and to be free of oppression.

Hands Up

'Hands Up' was created and performed by Abd Al Rahman Abu El-Qumboz, Yazan Sha'at and Ahmed Ashraf Kuhail from Al-Aqsa Elementary School B, a Ministry school in West Gaza with the help and support of their teacher, Ashraf Ahmed Kuhail. A recording of the play, performed by the actors is available here...

bit.ly/handsupAlaqsa

What the judges said: "Combines great comic acting and timing with a deadly serious message. Great effects and music."

Yazan: Hey Ahmed, look what I found!

Ahmed: Oh! What's this?

Yazan: It looks like a teapot, an old one.

Ahmed: Yuck! It's full of dust. Let me clean it.

Yazan: Oh my God! What's Happening?

Genie: Ahhhhh! *[Bellowing]* Who woke me up?

Yazan: Who are you?

Ahmed: And how did you get out of there?

Genie: Hey kids, don't waste my time. You know who I am. Don't tell me that you are from the Ice Age and have never seen me before.

Yazan: Are you the Genie?

Genie: No, I'm Rapunzel! Of course I'm. Ahhhhh! *[Bellowing]*) Come on, kids, tell me your wishes so I can make them come true.

Yazan: Anything?

Genie: Yeah.

Yazan: Hmmmm. Well I want to be famous, very famous.

Genie: Like Nick Bilbrough.

Yazan: Oh no, no. I want to have lots of cars, clothes and buildings ……… Oh wait… wait, I want to be rich… very rich…. I want to have lots of money.

Genie: Hello, Mr. Trump! You're just a young kid. Take this. *[hands him a lollipop]*

Ahmed: Don't be selfish! Think of others.

Yazan: Oh. Sorry! OK…I want to get my homeland, olive trees and holy places back.

Genie: Do you want to be millionaires or multi-millionaires?

Yazan: Are you making fun of us?

Genie: No. But I'm not strong enough to do such things.

Ahmed: OK. We want to travel.

Genie: To the Maldives!

Ahmed: No! Take us to Yemen, so we may wipe children's tears over there.

Yazan: Take us to Syria so we may help children keep safe from bombs.

Ahmed: Take us to Africa so we may help children to have food, water and to escape death.

Yazan: Take us all over the world to tell the children to raise their hands up and say "Enough! We are here! Please keep us out of your struggles. Please keep us safe."

Genie: Oh my God! You Palestinians are hard rocks! I confess that you are stronger than me and with such bravery you will make the impossible kneel and say "I surrender"… May Allah bless you Palestinians and make all of your wishes come true.

Yazan: Cease. Pray for peace.. pray for fire

Pray for love .. pray for every needy dove

Pray for happiness .. pray for forgiveness

Ahmed: Please keep us safe.

Yazan: We are still too young to go to our graves.

***

Ashraf says...

Unlike other children all over the world, Palestinian children grow abnormally with fear, depression, frustration, deprivation and with so many negative feelings. Gazan children, specifically, live in the biggest prison in the world. The Israeli siege on our borders and its successive wars may rank the children there as the most oppressed and disadvantaged anywhere in the world. I myself, as a father of four children, feel so bad towards my children when comparing them with other children in the world and even when comparing them with my wealthy, enjoyable and safe life in Saudi Arabia. I really feel sorry when I recall my amazing and beautiful memories there, and suddenly bump into those miserable ones of my own children. All of the above mentioned reasons were the strong motives that led me to write the play, Hands Up.

Hands Up was written with help of about 7 pupils who shared ideas and contributed in bringing its final version to fruition.

At first, the play's events were only about the Palestinian case, but one of the pupils suggested adding the suffering of similar children in countries of Yemen and Syria because he believed that they may not have the chance that the Hands Up project provides to express themselves and it would be great to do this on their behalf.

I Can Smell Her

'I Can Smell Her' was created and performed by Raghad Siam, Hala El-Hour, Eman Abed El-Razeq and Nour El-Mashharawi, from Gaza Elementary B School, with support from their teacher Sahar Siam. A recording of the play, performed by the actors is available here ...

bit.ly/icansmellher

What the judges said: "Highly innovative, original production, combining shadow theatre with close up acting. Explores loss in an unsentimental but deeply moving way."

Scene: *The stage is divided into two parts; the back section is a shadow theatre while the front section is a real stage.*

[Shadow stage. A girl stands up gradually in the centre]

Shadow girl: Darkness everywhere, but I can smell her. Yes…Be brave…Step forward.

[She falls down]

Shadow girl: No matter! No matter! I will stand again, but …

[The girl now appears on the real stage]

The girl: Shh.. shh …. Listen up! Can you hear?! Can you hear a very soft voice like the music of the morning; pretty enough to guide me towards…. *[She falls down]*

Shadow stage: *[An old man, holding a stick, walks slowly towards the girl].*

The old man: What are you doing? Take this stick; it will help you walk better.

The girl: A stick! I'm not blind. I can stare very well at everybody here. But I can't find her. Yet, I can smell her.

[Shadow stage: A woman, holding a plate, walks towards the girl]

The Woman: This is your lunch for today.

The girl: I don't want to eat, because it's really cool and tasteless. I want to be with her, since still I can smell her.

[A very loud explosion outside]

The girl: What happened? I am so afraid. These sounds are so scary. I've got a real bad need for you. Come here, can't you hear me?! How come? My face is like a pale ghost without you. I miss you, mum. But still I can smell you.

[The girl feels very cold… Shadow stage: A girl is holding a jacket]

The girl: No. No. It is still cool. I'll turn on the T.V. May her picture warm me.

[Shadow stage: Her mum works as a reporter.]

The girl: Mum! Love you mum! Miss you mum! Finally, I can see you!

[Strong explosion]

The girl: Oh my God! What's that? Mum ... No! No! No mum!

[she's crying]

[The first stanza of „My mum is amazing" song]

"She wakes up early in the morning with a smile

And she holds my head up high

Don't you ever let anybody put you down

Coz you are my little angel

Then she makes something warm for me to drink

Coz it's cold out there, she thinks

Then she walks me to school

Yes, I ain't no fool. I just think my Mom is amazing."

The girl: My mum was amazing. But she passed away. I will stand here alone; spray her perfume whenever I'd like to strengthen my resolve.

[Another girl, holding a picture, enters the stage]

Second girl: And I can see him whenever I'm about to lose my will, my father.

[A third girl, holding necklace, enters the stage]

Third girl: I can wear this, whenever I'd like to hug him – my brother.

[A fourth girl, holding a diary, enters the stage]

Fourth girl: I can read her words whenever I'd like to sleep with her – my mum.

The girl: Let's stay together …. 'till we can achieve our dreams.

All: Achieve our dreams.

***

Sahar says…

We joined the HUP in October 2018 because it is something very different from all what we, as teachers, have been doing for years. It is the first time for the students to contact people outside the besieged Gaza. This is not only about communication but also about developing students English fluency.

Gaza Elem. Girls (B) School drama club had a chance to contact with an Australian volunteer via zoom. Through weekly sessions students performed several plays and practiced various activities. Later this drama club started to brainstorm ideas and wrote short dialogues. They developed their own texts and finally produced the play "I can smell her". This play was very close to what has been inside their minds after 3 wars on Gaza. I mean it was about the inside fear of losing someone close to you and how we should support each other and not give up. Winning the competition was something monumental for those young girls when they felt that the message of resilience had been understood by the audience, and that they had made a play which could touch people. It enhanced the girls self-confidence and motivated them to dream bigger and do bigger.

One World, Different Stories

'One World, Different Stories' was created and performed by Deema Aljamal, Hala Hijazi, Iman Ridwan, Hala Nabaheen and Aseel El Khateeb from Al Rimal Prep Girls School B, UNRWA school, with support from their teacher, Amal Mukhairez. A recording of the play, performed by the actors is available here ...

bit.ly/oneworlddifferentdtories

What the judges said: "A tender rendition of yearning for humanitarian values in the face of oppression. Playful and committed acting."

Scene: *The play opens with a girl sneaking out of the shelter to play outside. Her friend joins her and they play together. Then, suddenly, one of the girls stops.*

[The musical background at the beginning of the play is taken from 'It Happened at al-Amiriyya', which was composed by an Iraqi musician after the bombing of an Iraqi shelter during the 1991 Gulf war. Over 400 Iraqis were killed, most of them children.]

Girl 1: Hey! Wait! We've got to go back to the shelter.

[Her friend seems indifferent]

Girl 2: No, let's play. Let's have fun.

Girl 1: *[grabbing her friend's hand]* Our mums must be worried now. Let's go back. Don't be silly.

Girl 2: *[insists]* No! Why not to be silly? There's nothing wrong with that.

Girl 1: It's not safe outside the shelter. Let's get inside quickly. It's safer there.

[Girl 1 drags her friend trying to get her inside the shelter, but Girl 2 resists when an explosion occurs. The two girls hug each other, then open their eyes slowly]

Girl 2: Oh! God! They bombed the shelter! Our shelter. *[She looks at her friend]* Didn't you say it was safer there?

Girl 1: Oh! Mum! Dad! My sisters! Oh, no.

Girl 2: We must leave this place.

Girl 1: What? Leave our homeland?

Girl 2: There's no place safe here. The dragon is sending its fire everywhere. Let's leave this piece of hell and head to dreamland.

Girl 1: Our dreamland. Yes, yes... a land where we can see blue skies, not orange ones. A land where we can hear birds, not shells. A land where we can see trees, not tanks. *[She looks at her friend]* Let's go.

Guard 1: *[angrily]* Where are you going?

Girl 1 and 2: *[together happily]* To dreamland!

Guard 2: *[haughtily]* Dreamland is not your land. You are not welcome here.

Guard 3: *[shouts]* Go back to your country!

Girl 1: *[sadly]* If our country was safe, we wouldn't leave.

Guard 1: We don't want you in our land. You are criminals! Terrorists!

Girl 2: *[shocked]* No! We are not!

Guard 2: *[arrogantly]* Look at yourself! You're ugly.

Guard 3: Go back! You're only a burden!

Girl 1: Not true! I'm going to find a job and work.

Guard 1: That's the problem. You're taking our jobs! You're taking our lives!

Guard 2: Go back!

Girl 2: But Earth belongs to everyone. It's not my fault I was born in that part of the world.

Girl 1: Yes! Can't we share the land, the food? Can't we share peace, love and joy?

Girl 2: We don't want to lead a dog's life anymore. War is a messy and ugly thing. I want to ride my bike again. I want my life back!

Guard 1: Look! I'm neither a leader, nor a billionaire. I can't help. I have orders. Go back!

[The girls try to talk to the guards again, but they take the three wise monkeys' position]

Girl 1: Please.. *[Guard 3 covers his ears]*

Girl 2: But let's .. *[Guard 2 covers his eyes]*

Girl 1: Can't we ... *[Guard 1 covers his mouth]*

[The girls turn to the audience]

Girl 2: You don't need to be a world to help others. Let's accept each other; let's help each other; let's look after each other.

Girl 1: Let's sit, talk, listen, hold hands, give hugs... Let's learn about other cultures, faiths and languages.

[Girl 2 takes the guards' hands away from their ears, eyes and mouth as she says..]

Girl 2: Give me your hand. Let's sprinkle kindness around. Remember one tiny action can make the world happier.

[The play ends with part of Charlie Chaplin's speech from The Great Dictator]

***

Amal says...

Drama is a wonderful tool that introduces our students to a world full of joy and play. It encourages them to push themselves to do something they thought was beyond their abilities. Whether they are behind the scenes or on stage, everyone has to come together to tell a story which can influence their well-being positively in different areas.

We started our drama club at school last year. Students from different levels joined the club and participated in many activities at school and outside the school. The Hands Up playwriting competition was one of the activities that my students wanted to take part in and they were getting ready for it even before it was officially announced.

Students worked on creating a good story that gripped people's attention and attracted them. They wanted their play to be understood and at the same time they wanted it to be very much related to their everyday life. So, they thought wars and refugees are issues that touch them and also matter to the whole world.

One World Different Stories is a play about two young refugees who have been forced to leave their homeland because of war and violence. They leave their country filled with hopes and dreams of a beautiful peaceful life, but they face rejection and negative attitudes towards them.

My students wanted to tell the story of every refugee, not only the story of the Palestinian refugees. They wanted to tell the world that being a refugee is not a decision we make; it's rather a choice between one horrible situation and a worse one. Through their play, they passionately try to tell the world the untold parts of their story as refugees.

The Hands Up playwriting competition is exactly what we need to convey messages of love, peace and empathy. It's our way to let the world see the big picture and listen to our part of the story.

The Living Song

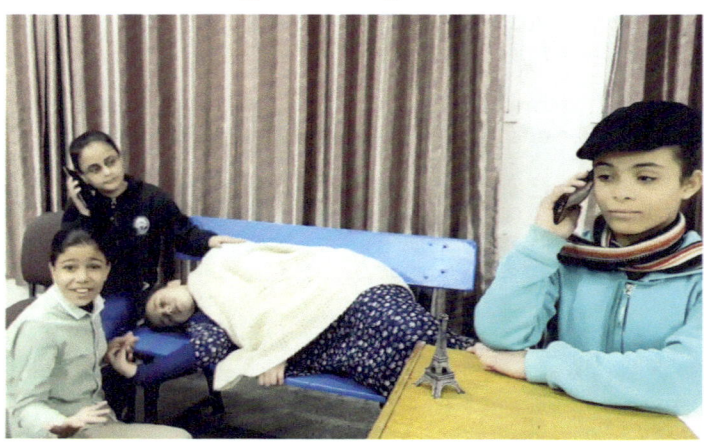

'The Living Song' was created and performed by Noha Al-Za'aneen, Hala Hamad, Yara Al-Sabe', Samah Naim and Ghazal Naseer from Beit Hanoun Elementary Co-ed "D" UNRWA School with support from their teacher, Hanaa Mansour. A recording of the play, performed by the actors is available here ...

bit.ly/thelivingsong

> *What the judges said: "A heart-warming portrayal of family life. Very smooth flow of interaction and scene changes."*

Scene 1: *A man is sitting on a table, and an Eiffel Tower model is on the table to indicate where he's living.*

Writer: Once upon a time there was a loving mother who looked after her 3 boys and a daughter. *[The writer leaves and takes the Tower model with him]*

[A card of the year 1995 is shown on the camera, and music is played]

Sami: *[a somehow selfish and jealous boy]* Mum, look isn't it beautiful? *[shows his drawing]*

Mum: Wonderful! But also you can do it better next time.

Sami: You always say that to me. It's nice, but do this. It's good, but do that.

Mum: That's because I want you to become better, my son.

Sami: *[not satisfied]* OK.

Mahmoud (a boy who is talented at writing): Mum, today I read the story I wrote, and guess what my teacher told me? That I'm going to have a bright future at writing.

Mum: I'm sure you will, dear. Keep on writing and practising.

Mahmoud: Of course, mum. Let's ask Ahmed. What does he have to tell us?

Sami: Mmmm ... Lots of nothings as usual.

Mum: Stop saying that to your brother. He has the kindest heart of you all and that's the most important thing.

[Mum stands and takes Ahmed to speak with him alone]

Mum: Don't be upset, my son.

Ahmed (a kind son): I'm not. I'm lucky to have you, mum.

Mum: What about you, naughty girl?

Reem (who is talented at singing): Well, well, well. I always sing at school and everyone is fascinated by my voice. And they always say that I'm going to be a famous singer having my own songs, doing interviews. I'm gonna be busy all the time. I'm already tired.

Mahmoud: OK, busy girl. Sing for us. You know writers get inspired by music.

Reem: No, I'm tired now.

Ahmed: I want your song, mum.

Reem: Not again. Mum keeps on singing it all the time. Didn't you get bored, mum?

Mum: *[stands up and says the words that she always says about her favourite song]* No, I'm not. I love this song. Actually, I adore this song. My grandmother used to sing it for my mother and my mother used to sing it for us. And here I am singing it for you. So I really wish this song will never die.

[The girl says her mum's words in a sarcastic way. She gets shy at the end when her mum realises she is being mocked]

Mum: Don't you like it? Maybe you will sing it for your children or an audience in the future?

Reem: I'm sure I won't. I'm gonna have my own modern songs.

Mum: OK, we will see.

Ahmed: So mum, sing it for us.

Mum: *[sings in Arabic and the translation is shown on a card]*

>I long for my mother's bread,

>my mother's coffee, and her touch.

Scene 2: *A card of the year 2018 is shown on the camera. The mother is lying and covered by a blanket and her kind son Ahmed is setting next to her.*

Ahmed: Where have you been all this time?

Sami: I was busy.

Ahmed: Doing what? No one knows, dear brother!

Sami: It's not your business.

Ahmed: Keep it quiet. Our mother's sleeping.

Sami: I think she's sleeping most of the time. So it's fine.

Ahmed: Not going to reply. *[He leaves]*

[Sami takes photos of his mother with his mobile and writes on his Facebook page]

Sami: "Pray for my mother. She's old and sick. Can't leave her for a moment."

[He looks over his Facebook and notices his sister's interview.]

Sami: Come and see your sister. She's in a show now.

[A card of the show 'Our Night with the Star' is presented to the camera]

Interviewer: This is the end of our program. What would you like to sing for us?

Reem: I'd love to end with a very special song to me. I've never thought how much it really means to me.

Interviewer: Please, start.

[Reem sings her mother's song in Arabic and the translation is shown]

Reem: My childhood memories grow within me. Day after day. I love my life because if I died, I would be truly embarrassed by my mother's tears.

[The writer sits on the table, putting back the Eiffel Tower, and writes]

Mahmoud the writer: The girl sang and inside she wished that her mum could see and listen to her, singing her favourite song in front of the whole world and hoping that this song would never die as her mum had dreamed. The End.

[He takes his phone and calls his brother Ahmed.]

Ahmed: *[Completely thrilled]* She smiled.

Sami: *[Truly moved and pleased]* Our mum smiled.

Ahmed: I think she remembered the song.

Mahmoud the writer: I wish I could be there with you all.

***

Hanaa says...

"Other things may change us, but we start and end with the family", as Anthony Brandt stated. When I saw my girls presenting a simple, yet very heart-warming still image showing a portrayal of family life during applying some drama club activities, the idea of creating a play about family sparkled in our minds.

After a fruitful discussion about the represented images, we agreed to work on the family image to start our play. I believe most of us saw their parents, siblings, and their normal family life in that image. Most of us were raised listening to our mothers singing chants or songs; thus, our play is entitled The Living Song.

Contributing to the remote theatre competition and being one of the finalists has been a great experience for the girls. Improving their confidence at speaking out their ideas, becoming familiar with more vocabulary, and most importantly, raising their awareness and responsibility are clearly the benefits of enrolling my girls in the competition. Indeed, we teachers aim to prepare our students to be more articulate, confident and creative citizens of this world. Such an experience definitely helps in that aim.

The Shadow Girl

'The Shadow Girl' was created and performed by Nagham Abu Al-Oun, Haya Orouq, Nada Hijazi, Sarah Abu Hwidi and Abeer Al-Khatib from Asma Prep B Girls UNRWA school with support from their teacher, Haneen Khaled. A recording of the play, performed by the actors is available here...

bit.ly/theshadowgirlUNRWA

What the judges said: "A beautifully choreographed play about the dangers of social media addiction."

<u>Scene One:</u> *We meet three girls who represent the social media. And one girl who is going to use these social media tools in the shadow "not real".*

Narrator: *[musical tone and the shadow girl walks behind]* Once, there was a girl who had nothing meaningful in her life.

She looked around for someone to care

For real things to share.

But all around was a space

…. and suddenly there were three girls.

Her focus was narrow.

So she decided to live with them as a shadow.

[The three girls talk to the shadow girl and present themselves to her]

Girl 1 (Facebook): *[catches the shadow girl's hand]* Here I am, the Facebook. So let us have a look. You can upload your life events and get likes, comments and notifications. I'm with you if you are at home, work or even on vacation.

Girl 2 (Whatsapp): *[entering the stage from the other side and catching her other hand]* Whatsapp, whatsapp, talk ..talk .. talk. You can chat every morning; you can chat every day; you can chat when it is dark and when it is light. I mean you can use me all the day and all night.

Girl 3 (Instagram): *[entering the stage from behind]* Give me your shining photos. Bring me your beautiful acts. You can share your birthday with cakes and sweets. You can upload your favourite dish of meat and even you can share your moments with family and friends, mum, dad and kids.

[sad music and the shadow girl is talking now and moving ahead approaching the front of the stage]

Girl 4 (The shadow girl): *[sad tone]* You are so amazing to use, but what if I don't have anything to share, no friends to care and no family to sit with; only time that can be described with one word, 'spare'. *[She stretches her hands right and left and closes her eyes with sadness]*

Scene Two: *The three girls are trying to persuade the shadow girl to use them despite all this.*

Girl 1 (Facebook): *[hitting her gently to make her wake up]* You don't have to have real ones. Just come and post and you will see millions who care about you.

Girl 2 (Whatsapp): I'm the best for you. With me, you can have friends to talk with and spend your time.

Girl 3 (Instagram): *[with a hug]* Imagine your lovely moments and just click 'upload'. Don't be so sensitive, dear.

Girl 1, Girl 2, Girl 3: *[all have a big hug with the shadow girl]* We are all near.

Girl 4: *[happily moves to change the background scenery]* Oh, let's share, let's comment, let's chat. Let us imagine a life full of colours and dollars. I have to enjoy my life on the screens. I don't care.

All four girls: *[happily flying around the stage and waving their hands above heads]* Heeeey!

Girl 4 (The shadow girl): *[clicking]*

[with Facebook] like

[with Instagram] upload

[with Whatsapp] chat

[the three girls are jumping with happiness]

Scene Three: *The electricity goes off and all the social media has stopped working.*

[Girl 1, 2, and 3 are on the ground now with heads down]

Narrator: *[musical tone]*

The electricity went out.

She stared and started to shout.

She was in pain,

for everything had gone, in vain.

Girl 4 (Shadow girl): *[talking to the three girls with anger]* Darkness! What happened to you all? You are not working and not moving at all!

Girl 4: *[talking to Facebook girl angrily]* I want to see how many likers there are. *[to the Instagram girl]* And how many comments on my last birthday photos? *[and to the Whatsapp girl, begging]* Please show me how many chats are waiting for me?

[The girls don't move at all because there is no electricity]

Girl 4 (The shadow girl) *[looking carefully at the audience]* Oh, I was living in the shadow and shadow leads to darkness one day. Facebook, Whatsapp, Instagram. I became an unreal girl. I'm a shadow girl because all this happening to you is fake. It is like rain that disappears with the sun shines.

[Thee three girls 1, 2, and 3 are off stage now]

Girl 4 (the shadow girl): *[with a shining background]* Now, it is my time to shine and search for real friends, real people and a real world.

[The shadow girl is off the stage now and the narrator enters]

Narrator: *[singing]* Social media allows masks and lies.

We need real people in front of our eyes.

<u>*The final scene:*</u> *the four girls together enter the stage as real friends, not as social media devices and they sing the ending song.*

[The four girls and the narrator singing]

Let's be together forever and ever *[twice]*

We need to be real

Not to be fake

It is not on the screens

It is by the good things we make

***

Haneen says...

I couldn't ever imagine that my young learners in Gaza could manage to write a play in a language that is not their mother tongue. It was really a massive challenge, but surprisingly they did this amazingly and made it to the finals.

We made the play because we are part of the Hands Up Project family, and we wanted to send a message to the world that social media makes us very distant from each other. We become mechanical more than emotional. Also, it is not always true, as many people live in the shadow of its mask.

I held a lot of meetings with drama club members for remote theatre, training and informing them of all the principles of entering the competition. The students were very excited by this. All the drama club members gathered to give ideas that we could work on later on. Then, we decided to make it about social media because it is the language of today's life. Regarding the selection of the five students, five students showed their passion and creativity towards this project, so they were selected .They worked day and night, supported by me, to write the script, rehearse it and then perform it. We spent two months of training and then 4 hours of documenting it as a video track of 5 minutes to get it to England.

This experience covered all aspects of language learning. The students wrote and created a masterpiece that was not in their mother tongue. I think it was more than beneficial. Working on such a process helped them to live with the language and move them forward in their fluency.

Thank you all for making this come true!

Don't Look Back

'Don't look back' was created and performed by Dania Dahalan, Sara Dahalan and Roze Al Sa'doni from New Khan Younis Prep Girls UNRWA school, Gaza, with support from their teacher, Abeer Awad. A recording of the play, performed by the actors is available here...

bit.ly/dontlookbackUNRWA

What the judges said: "Using the screen cleverly as a magic mirror, this is an enchanting, original fairy tale. Powerful, close up acting."

Scene: *The two little girls enter their parent's bedroom which has been closed for a long time.*

Rose: Finally we enter our mum's bedroom.

Dania: I don't know why she's kept it closed all this time?

Rose: It's so dark.

Dania: Look! It's mum's stuff.

Rose: I can't see anything. Where's the light?

Dania: Here.

Rose: Cool, let's play with it.

Dania: No, No, No. We will wait until she's back home after work.

Rose: It's OK. Please. Come on.

Dania: I don't know I'm …… *[Rose interrupts]*

Rose: No one will get hurt.

Dania: Just look, OK.

Rose: Yes! *[excited]*

Dania: Be careful! *[looking at something]*

Rose: What's this thing? *[astonished]*

Dania: It's a mirror, can't you see?

Rose: I can, but it looks different.

Dania: I know.

Rose: Wow! It's very big. *[surprised]*

Dania: Look! There's something written here: „Mirror, mirror on the wall, open shine in the hall'! What does that mean?

Rose: Why then did you read it?

[A voice comes out from the mirror; girls are shocked]

Dania: What's this? Who are you?

Magic mirror: I'm the magic mirror, I'm the only one.

Tell me anything and I'll make it done.

Rose: Amazing! Are you real? Like real? Can I have a wish?

Dania: Seriously! You can see it, so it's real.

Rose: So we have a wish.

Dania: We should use it well *[excited]*

Rose: Dania, can I start please?

Dania: Whatever. What do you wish?

Magic mirror: Come on, little one, tell me. What do you want?

Rose: Mmm …, I …. I wanna a teddy a bear.

Dania: What an important wish! *[ironically]*.

Magic mirror: Your wish will become real. Stay here and don't have any fear.

Rose: *[staring at the bear]* Cool. Oh, it looks like the old one which dad brought me on my sixth birthday.

Dania: Let me see. Yes, you're right. Rose, do you remember our father..? *[sadly]*

Rose: Yes, he was an amazing man and he cared about everyone.

Dania: He promised to stay with us but he ………..

Rose: *[interrupts]* Come on.

Dania: Now I understand why mum keeps it closed all that time. All her memories have been hidden here in this room.

Rose: What's your wish?

Dania: I have a lot of questions and wonder so much about life, but I guess we should use our wishes for dreams only.

Rose: Just try.

Dania: Why are our souls cheap while the others in the world are not? Why do we have to live this hard life? Our dad went and he never came back. What was his fault when he was killed in the war? What was our fault in losing him? ... Lots of questions, but l guess you, mirror, cannot answer me. Why do we have to live like this? *[the girls collapse]*

Magic mirror: My sweet girl, maybe l cannot answer you. But never give in to that idea; don't allow your past to control your present or your future. Whatever happened, you must let it go. Leave the pain of your past behind, so it cannot ruin your future. Leave the darkness of your life behind, so it cannot block the light of your bright future. Your past is gone. Don't allow the events of the past which are now gone to ruin this moment which is perfect; this moment which is now to enjoy; which is ready for you to live fully. And remember: good things may come to those who wait.

[in this scene, the big sister (Dania) thinks deeply of the speech of the mirror while Rose is crying]

Dania: No, No, Rose. As we are still alive, we never give up hope. One day we will be happy.

Rose: We're strong, aren't we?

Dania: Yes, dear. *[a great hug between them]*

Magic mirror: The Magic mirror is leaving now. I hope your wondering is over somehow

[girls look to the mirror as it disappears]

Dania: Never forget.

[the two sisters sing their song]

We're together sisters forever,

nothing will lead us back,

we're so close,

our life and souls,

Life will go on.

***

Abeer says...

Being Palestinian means you are not like other citizens of any country in this world. We have gone through many hardships; many children have lost their loved ones - mums or dads - in wars. Those children may grow up hopeless or may live an ordinary life but for sure with always a question in their minds: „WHY ME?!"

WHY did I lose my loved ones?

Our children want to live happily and safely like others around the world. So I asked the students to focus on the things that inspire hope. Despite suffering, oppression or anything bad that happens to us, we shouldn't give up and must try to look for happiness.

My students and I discussed the ideas together; then they really started writing. Dania, my amazing student, suggested the idea of the mirror of life in the play. We discussed how this mirror could lead the heroines of the play towards the truth, and could succeed in convincing them not to look back but move forward. This is the basic message we wanted to convey in this play.

Dania, Sara and Roze were enthusiastic and highly motivated to participate in the competition. They tried their hardest, and after a lot of intensive training, they did a great performance.

This experience helped them a lot to develop their English language skills. Indeed they became more confident in communicating with others, and expressing themselves well using facial expressions and body language.

Hands Up Project helps us – both teachers and students - to boost our ability in acting, to produce our fantasy in drama and then change it into reality.

The Nightmare

'The Nightmare' was created and performed by Fatema Alzahra Khaled Zeidat, Sofia Bahjat Zeidat and Sabreen Mohammad Zeidat from Shuhada' Bani Nae'm Basic School, Hebron, Palestine with support from their teacher, Maisoon Zeedat. A recording of the play, performed by the actors is available here ...

bit.ly/thenightmareSBNBS

What the judges said: "A play showing the importance of parents valuing their children. Extremely strong acting, humorous and believable.

Scene: *Opens with the sound of a broken glass, and then an angry mother appears looking for her daughter, Sarah.*

Mother: Hey Sarah, where are you? What did you break? Stop that. Come here, Sarah. Show me your face.

[Sarah appears afraid and worried]

Sarah: I'm here, mom, I'm here.

[The mother is holding Sarah's ear firmly]

Mother: Aren't you ashamed of yourself? You've made a mess of the house. What a naughty girl.

Sarah: Mom, I didn't break the glass. It fell by itself.

Mother: Listen, I warn you. That's the last time. I want my house to be clean and tidy all the time. You broke all the cups and glasses; you poured juice on the carpet. Not only that, you play and throw your toys everywhere. You don't deserve such a house to live in. You are like a monkey jumping from place to place. Don't you ever get tired?

Sarah: Sorry, mom, I won't repeat it. I want to play. I feel bored. I can't keep quiet all the time. Do you want me to be silent all the time?

Mother: Yes, a good daughter is the one who listens to her mother.

Sarah: OK, mom, I will try to be as you want me. Eating, observing, sitting on the sofa, doing homework and sleeping.

[Sarah collapses and becomes unconscious]

Mother: Sarah, What's wrong with you? Do you hear me? Oh, God, I must take her to the hospital.

[The mother takes Sarah quickly to the hospital]

Mother: Oh, God! Please, heal my daughter.

[The doctor comes]

Mother: Doctor, please tell me, is Sarah OK? What's wrong with her?

Doctor: I'm sorry to tell you that she has cancer and won't live long. So you have to take care of her in her last few days.

[The doctor goes out, leaving the mother shocked]

Mother: Cancer, cancer! This is the last thing that I expected. So does this mean my house will lose Sarah? Does this mean I will live alone in this life? I don't want my house to be tidy all the time. Sarah, Sarah, come here throw your toys everywhere.

[The mother leaves and Sarah enters]

Sarah: Hey mom, where are you? I was late to school. Oh, this is the first time my mom didn't wake me up early. It's 8 o'clock. Hey mom, wake up, wake up.

[The mother comes. She has been sleeping. She looks surprised at her daughter and starts thinking and remembering. She looks at Sarah, turns her around, checking her]

Mother: Sarah, are you OK? Aaah. It was a dream. I was dreaming. It was a nightmare.

[She hugs Sarah firmly and kisses her]

[Sarah is surprised that her mother is not as she used to be]

Sarah: It's strange - my mother has gone crazy. She usually shouts at me in the morning. What's she planning to do? Mom, are you okay? I must go to school. Goodbye.

Mom: Goodbye Sarah, take care of yourself, love you.

[Sarah leaves]

Mother: Thank you, God, that Sarah is okay and doesn't have cancer. Even though it was a dream, it taught me a lesson: love your children. Let their smile abide everywhere. Don't deprive them, because you never know when you might lose them. Teach them to be correct in their life. Remember, a warm word in their life is better than a kiss on a dead body.

***

The Nightmare

Maisoon says...

When I learned about remote theatre competition, I told my students. They liked the idea very much. They discussed what to act and they chose the topic - The Nightmare. They acted this play with my help and support.

The Nightmare aims to express many goals. It focuses on the value of things after we lose them by using an example of a mother who deals badly with her daughter. But while she is sleeping she has a nightmare and that changes her outlook completely. And she changes her way of dealing with her children.

My students enjoyed this experience very much and they are ready to compete again and act more beautiful English plays. Moreover, they have more self confidence in using English. Great thanks to Hands Up Project for this amazing competition.

Don't Kill the Olive

'Don't Kill the Olive' was created and performed by Sarah Alhamarnan, Bayan Mahdi Abed and Seba Ismael from Maghazi Prep Girls School, Gaza with support from their teacher, Hanan Hamouda Abu Mashayekh. A recording of the play, performed by the actors is available here ...

http://bit.ly/dontkilltheolive

What the judges said: "A play about the way family values have broken down because of addiction to technology. Well-acted and very topical."

Scene One: *A daughter comes back from school extremely happy and is talking to her mother with joy in her voice. The mother is too occupied with her mobile phone that she cannot even notice her girl or respond to her.*

Daughter: Mum ..Mum... I'm home. You won't believe it. My teacher has chosen me to sing a song on Mother's Day. She said I have a fascinating voice. I'm very happy, mum. *[mother still occupied with her mobile phone and social media]*

Daughter: Mum., would you please help me to practise? Mum... mum... Can you hear me? Mum ... mum.

Mother: *[in a very angry tone]*) Shut up. Can't you see? I'm very busy, go away.

Daughter: But I need your help!

Mother: *[shouting]* Not now .. I am online.

[Daughter starts to practice singing alone with sadness in her voice]

Scene Two: *Daughter comes in with a small olive in her hands. Her mother, as usual, is busy on her mobile phone*

Daughter: Oh my beloved mum, look at my new science project. It's a small olive sapling. I'm going to plant it and take care of it till it grows and becomes a tree.. Oh! I can imagine how big it will be. It will give us the best olive oil. Do you know that olive oil is the healthiest .... Mum, can you hear me? I need your help ... Mum .. look how beautiful it is.

Mother: *[takes the sapling out of her daughter's hands and throws it away shouting]* Get out you noisy girl... Can't you see I'm busy? You're annoying me.

[The daughter is shocked and breaks down, on her knees]

[At this point, the image of the mother and daughter freezes, a narrator comes in and looks at both of them, refusing to accept what has just happened]

Narrator: Inside each one of our children, there is a small olive sapling that needs care and love ... Please, don't kill the olive sapling.

Scene Three: *The play goes back to the start point again, but this time with a change in attitude.*

Daughter: Mum ..Mum... I'm home, you won't believe it. My teacher has chosen me to sing a song on Mother's Day. She said I have a fascinating voice. I'm very happy, mum.

Mother: Oh, my dear baby.. Let's listen to your amazing voice.

***

Hanan says...

It was an amazing experience. The moment I heard about the playwriting and performing competition within the Hands Up Project, I launched one of my own at my school. I received many beautiful plays and so, I gathered the members of the English Drama club and discussed the entries. To be honest, we all fell in love with .. Don't kill the olive .. by Sarah Alhamarna from the first read (if we can say so).

Choosing actors was another significant experience. I was looking for a neglected daughter and a tough careless mother; students needed to be able to convey the main idea of the play using their voices and limited movements in front of a stationary mobile phone camera. It was not an easy mission, and yet it was very unique.

We were very happy when we started to practise performing the scenes of the play. we all went through some amazing moments. My students became less shy, more confident with their language, voices and movements; they learned more about symbolism, which in turn helped them to act better.

Even though .. Don't kill the olive .. was not one of the finalists, it is a very good play. I was confident of that, especially when I read your feedback about it. I am sure that we will be better next year, as long as we avoid our mistakes and work harder on our flaws.

The Power of Words

'The Power of Words' was created and performed by Rawan El Bahnasawi, Dana Nawas, Raghad El Na'ami, Heba Jaber and Nada El Khatib from Nuseirat Prep. "A" Girls UNRWA School in Gaza with support from their teacher, Mariam Abu Seifan. A recording of the play, performed by the actors is available here ...

bit.ly/thepowerofwordsNuseirat

What the judges said: "A passionately acted play about how words can devastate or encourage young aspirations."

Characters: **Victoria Smith, Mum, The computer expert, Victoria's friend, Rose** *and* **The company representative**

Scene one

Victoria: You know, I feel that I have abilities and I'm so skilful.

Rose: Come on! You should finish your studies first. Then, talk about your skills.

Victoria: You will see. Give me your laptop.

Rose: *[reads something on the laptop]* Oh!!!!! $7000!

Victoria: What! What!

Rose: Shhh. It's a prize from Google or Joojle company for the one who can program a certain computer program. I can't read it correctly.

Victoria: Oh! Wow! I've been waiting for this. I'm going to win.

[Rose leaves the room; Victoria works on her laptop]

Scene two

Mum: *[angrily]* Oh my God! You spend all your time on this machine loptap or laptop. Be careful about your studies. Idiot… daft …. Don't you have the sense to think of your future? Offfff ..

Victoria: Mum, mum.

Mum: Yes, Victoria.

Victoria: *[very afraid]* I need 10 shekels to buy something.

Mum: Oh no, 10 shekels …… money. You don't succeed, or work and you want money!

Victoria: Calm down. Calm down. I don't want money. Calm down.

[alone and very sad] I don't deserve money. I don't deserve life. I won't participate in the competition. I won't study. I am a failure. No one loves me. I will escape from this bad world.

Scene three

Rose: Victoria, the computer expert is waiting for you.

Victoria: What?! Let him come in, quickly.

Rose: OK.

[The computer expert enters]

Victoria: Welcome, welcome. Sit down here, please.

The computer expert: I want to teach you how to programme certain things as your computer teacher told me. Time is short, so let's start.

[The expert teaches her]

The computer expert: We have finished. Your computer teacher told me about your difficult conditions at home. Listen to me carefully. You should study hard and work on your program as well. You can do it.

Scene four

[Victoria is studying hard and working on her programme]

Victoria: *[Happily]* I have finished my final exams. Now, I've finished the program, I'll send it. Enter ...

My God, I worked hard – day and night. I afford all the bad words. Help me God. Success is what I seek.

Mum: Again, again this laptop! Can't you understand?! You're going to fail again and again. I don't want to see this laptop any more.

Victoria: No, no. Don't break it. Don't break it. [Mum breaks the laptop] Why? Why my laptop? Why my laptop? Why? Why?

Rose: Victoria, congrats. You succeeded and got 95 percent.

Victoria: What! *[Victoria and Rose hug each other]*

Mum: What happened?

Victoria: I succeeded.

Mum: Congrats. *[Mum and Victoria hug each other]*

Scene five

The company representative: Where's Victoria Smith?

Victoria: I'm here. *[looks surprised]*

The company representative: Congratulations! You won the competition and got $7000. *[She gives Victoria a cheque]*

Victoria: What! Thank you, thank you. Thank God.

[She gives the cheque to her mum]

Mum: Oh! My daughter, forgive me, forgive me. I treated you so badly. I didn't support you. I'm sorry. I'm really sorry. [Mum cries]

Victoria: It's OK, mum. I love you. *[Mum throws the cheque away. She hugs her daughter]*

Victoria: *[to the audience]* And to you, I want to say: The impact of words on people is incredible.

The real power is in the words we use. Encouraging words cost nothing, but they can make all the difference to someone.

***

Mariam says...

Our play came from a real story. Dana's (the writer of the play) brother has a friend who suffers from difficult conditions at home. His father travelled for work and he stayed with his mother. His mother was very tough with him. I liked the idea as it reflects an important social aspect: the relationship between parents and children. We changed the story a little, e.g. a girl instead of a boy. Dana wrote the play and I gave some language support. This is what the girls said about the experience:

Dana: "Really, drama helps me to write English. I learned many new words. Doing plays was how I started and now I have written one. It's incredible - drama has always helped me to achieve more. I participated in a local free composition competition. I won and got the first place A+. Without drama and the help of Mrs. Mariam Siefan, I wouldn't have achieved that. Honestly, I can't imagine my life without such experiences.

Rawan: "I do believe that drama helps in reshaping my character. I became braver. I'm not shy anymore. Also, this play changed my beliefs. I'm a nervous person and sometimes I shout. The message of this play has become a golden rule in my life: 'Encouraging words cost nothing but they can make all the difference to someone'."

Nada: "Drama affects my character positively. I made many new friends. I rehearse and act new plays in a local centre. I won't stop. These two plays are the first of many. Drama is just amazing!"

Raghad : "I'm fond of the English language. Drama is a powerful tool for me to practice and speak English fluently. I improved my accent as well. I became able to speak English with feeling rather than speaking like a robot. Loads of thanks to the Hands up Project for this chance."

Chapter 3
The Right to Participation

The Right to Participation is the right of any child to participate (dependent on that child's age and maturity), either directly or indirectly, in decisions that affect his or her future and well-being. When you are faced with severe obstacles and limitations on your aspirations, as Palestinian children are, it is vital to feel you have some control over your future. We see this theme of self-determination in **It's Your Choice and I Can**. In **Who's the Master** and **The Sky's Your Limit** an internal battle between doubts and hope is played out, while in **Success Story** and **The Lord of the Show** we are shown models of hope, first in an example of someone striving alone to overcome difficulties and in the latter in an example of successful team work. The message in **Hand in Hand** is to look to the future and not dwell on the past. **Tell Me Why** questions why children have to be faced with such limitations to their dreams in the first place.

Hand in Hand

'Hand in Hand' was created and performed by Roaa Radwan, Yaqeen Asfour, Sarah Abu Dagga and Tala Brim from Abasan Prep Girls School, UNRWA school Gaza Strip, Khan Younis with the help and support of their teacher, Amani Kullab. A recording of the play, performed by the actors is available here...

bit.ly/handinhandAbasan

What the judges said: "Challenges the idea of dwelling too much on the past. Passionately acted and sung."

Scene: *Laila enters the stage, walking in the forest singing; then is shocked by the sight of three girls sitting in black clothes*

Laila: Who are you? Are you humans or ghosts? Speak, please. You are scaring me.

Tala: Do not be scared, Laila. We are humans just like you.

Laila: Why are you hiding your faces? Closing your eyes?

Yaqeen: Nothing deserves to be seen in this world and no one can see us.

Laila: Your clothes .. Why are they colourless? Where are the colours?

Sarah: We do not want different colours, different faces or different clothes. When we become the same there will be justice and no one will feel jealous of the others. We are all the same.

Laila: Why do you keep away from other people?

Tala: It is not safe to live with them. They became tough without feelings, kindness or mercy. They fight and kill each other. There is no love in this world.

Laila: NO .. This is not true. We still have family, relatives and friends who love us, care about us.

Yaqeen: Love is a part of the past buried for a long, long time. Our minds are full of terrible moments which should be deleted.

Laila: But also we have beautiful moments with happy times we spent with our families. Times we laughed, ran, played and danced.

Sarah: What about moments of fear and wars? Moments of killing and destroying?

Laila: We can stop them all.

Tala: We need to go back in time to delete all moments of fear and war. Maybe when we go back in time I can find my grandfather who went and never came back. Maybe my grandma can stop singing for the absent sons to come back. Maybe my uncle has two legs now and my father can live among us today to wipe away my tears.

By going back in time children may live with their families and everyone can have a home. We may see smiling faces and kindness in hearts. Our birds fly and sing for love and freedom. And that old olive tree hugs my house shadow every morning to celebrate love and peace. Wars have not occurred. Homes have not been destroyed. Dreams are still alive. No fears.. No tears.. No bombs.. No rockets shining in the sky that take everyone dear to my heart.. Who knows..? Maybe...

Laila: *[talks to herself]* But we cannot go back in time and delete all bad memories and scenes of horror and fear.

Sarah: So we will stay away from other people. *[sits down]*

Laila: You decided to give up and lose all the meanings on humanity we still have.

Tala: There is nothing we can do.

Laila: You can do a lot. If you still have the desire to change, the love in your heart, then you can...

Yeqeen: It is difficult.

Laila: But it is not impossible. Face the world. Talk to people. Every one of them has a beautiful dream inside him. With hope we can wake up charity inside hearts. With love we can colour their life with beauty. With faith we can make them believe in themselves. Work together hand in hand to make a difference. This is the only way, believe me.

[Laila starts to remove the black covers, replacing them with colourful ones and singing with them]

Open your eyes look around

Watch the blue, the flying birds

The green trees, the smiling rose

Feel the life with shining rays

All the dark soon disappear

Hold the hope and raise your dream

Hold the flag, don't be afraid

***

Amani says...

Hand in Hand is a reflection of the dark life everyone lives in Gaza or it could be in any other place in the world with a similar situation. People have suffered for generations and faced a very difficult life. Men and women, old and young, they are all tired and depressed. Everyone has lost a dear one or missed home. Everyone has identified fear in the early stages and we need help from people all over the world. This why we made the play.

At the beginning when I gathered my students to choose a topic to talk about, everyone had a problem related to her own life and wanted to talk about it. So, I tried to include all of them in one scene within five minutes and it was not easy. The special idea was to make a mixture between children's lives in Palestine and magic stories that all children like. This is why the girls chose Leila (Little Red Riding Hood) as a famous character to find the children in the forest and try to help and lead them to love, hope and faith, as a solution to face life and make a difference.

My students worked hard to convey their message and they did it. This successful experience led them to think seriously how to make their words louder and stronger in other upcoming plays. Through Hands Up Project we could go beyond any political borders and talk about our situation. Thank you, Mr. Nick, from the depth of my heart. We really feel grateful.

I Can

'I Can' was created and performed by Basem Hijazi, Mahmoud Al Ghalban and Abd Alrahman Abu Ajlan from Mae'n Prep Boys School, Gaza with support from their teacher, Imad Wahba. A recording of the play, performed by the actors is available here...

bit.ly/2koqhfT

What the judges said: "A very moving take on how hope and effort can overcome external limitations. Powerful physical theatre."

Scene: *A black curtain with some drawings of abstract art refers to the real situation in Gaza. Some things like a rubbish basket and a broom refers to the mess in Gaza.*

[A sound of cheerful music. Actor A enters the stage slowly from a corner and raises his arms as if he is flying. He performs a dance according to the development of music]

[He stops dancing gradually and puts his hand over his eyebrows as if he is looking for something far away. Then he smiles]

A: I could see them .. I could see them.. Ya..oh ..I could see them...

[He looks around and doesn't find his friend. He calls aloud to them]

A: But.. where are you, my dear friends?

B & C: *[From the wings]*

B: We are here *[they appear while A keeps looking into the distance]*

C: I can't see anything.

B: What are you looking at?

A: *[He points with his finger]*

A: Wow .. look at our dreams there.. They are coming around ..Can you see?

B: *[Mocking]* Yeah..yeah.. they are coming ..they are coming.. Just step forward to look clearly for them.

[A steps forward just one step. B hits him on the nape of his neck]

B: This is just to look good .. What dreams are you talking about? Dear, here in Gaza, don't dream .. because dreams here are dying.

A: Why? *[Screaming with a sad voice] [soft music]* Hey .. Tell me why ? Listen .. I can become a doctor.

B: *[he puts the wooden barrier and sign "NO Jobs"]*

A: OK..OK .. Listen .. I can live here peacefully.

B: *[he puts the wooden barrier and sign "3 wars in 10 years"]*

A: OK.. OK .. I can travel.. Yes, I can travel.

B: *[He puts the wooden barrier and sign "Border Closed"]*

A: OK.. I can .. I can … *[in a loud voice]*

A: I can … *[B puts the Wooden barrier "No permission/entry"]*

[Actor A disappears behind the barriers and they cover his whole body]

[The music comes to an end]

[B is looking towards the actor and ties his hands]

[Silence for a few seconds]

[A sound of full challenging music plays from a low volume until it comes up and up. Lights start to flash on and off]

[Actor A's body doesn't appear opposite the camera until he hits all the signs right and left. Finally his hand appears when he breaks through the last sign and he starts to tear the paper of the barrier; then his body appears gradually until he gets through the barrier]

[He comes closer to the camera shouting loudly and written on his outstretched arms is "I am a Human"]

[The challenging music continues until the end]

[Actor A comes closer and closer to the camera until the end of the shot]

***

Imad says...

When we first started writing such a play, we dreamt about a piece of theatre that could encounter all the challenges that could stop producing this work. We started thinking of a play that could reflect the suffering of people who reside in the largest prison in the world, but not in a crude way. I thought of the Hands Up Project (HUP) as an excellent means of delivering this message to the world.

We started forming the essence of the play by consulting the daily problems in the news. Hence, the idea emerged and that beautiful body of art started to be formed. I trained my students whose first time it was acting in a play and they were very enthusiastic during the rehearsals.

We, the team of the play, used the simplest scenery of the play that could be used and we also made use of the school furniture. In fact, we made everything out of nothing.

The great success of the play is that we came up with what the play had targeted. Actually, the great benefit was the new spirit of hope that my students acquired when they achieved this breakthrough.

It's Your Choice

'It's Your Choice' was created and performed by Malak Radi, Yasmine Jouda, Noor Hijazi, Malak Abu Safi and Lama Abu Ouda from Beach Prep Girls' School 'C', Gaza with support from their teacher Abeer Younis. A recording of the play, performed by the actors is available here ...

bit.ly/2lDKWww

What the judges said: "A play within a play that reflects on modern society, using Cinderella's shoes as a metaphor. Classy, engaging and inspiring."

Narrator: Sara and Huda are best friends. Today, there's a big party in their school, and now, they are watching the play of "Cinderella". They seem very excited.

[The curtains are opened and Cinderella appears dancing and singing "Lavender"]

Lavender's blue dilly dilly, Lavender's green

When I am king dilly dilly, you shall be queen

[The prince enters. She stops when she sees him]

The prince: Who are you?

Cinderella: I'm Cinderella, Majesty. I'm not a princess. I have no parents.

The prince: It's OK. Will you try this? *[He refers to the shoe]*

Cinderella: Yes, Majesty. *[Cinderella tries the shoe and it fits her. Both of them seem happy.]*

The prince: You're my princess. I promise to make you happy.

[The audience clap happily. Both the prince and Cinderella come closer to greet the audience]

Narrator: Huda and Sara like the play so much as they live a very hard life like Cinderella. But will they have a happy ending like Cinderella? Let's see! *[Huda and Sara enter. They seem happy]*

Sara: Oh! What a beautiful play!

Huda: Yes, I like it. It's amazing.

Sara: I hope to have a rich and beautiful prince like Cinderella. Someone who saves me from this miserable life.

Huda: *[ironically]* Huhhh ... Save you?! Can you imagine how many Cinderellas there are in the world ..... Hundreds?........ Thousands? .....Millions? .... and two. *[she refers to herself and Sara, and smiles)* And how many princes are there? .... You're dreaming.

Huda: Hey you...........

Sara: Oh! Stop it, Huda. You're boring. Guess what! I'll do my best to get a prince..... so... First, I must buy beautiful shoes to be ready. You'd better come with me.

Huda: Of course I won't...... I won't wait for a superhero to save me. No one can change my life EXCEPT ME. I'll finish my studies and work hard to make my life better. Then I'll have my own business, and I'll have whatever I want. I'm sure I will.

Sara: *[ironically]* You know, I can ask my prince to give you a job.

Huda: No dear. Thanks for your great offer.

Sara: Oh, there's no time; I have many things to do. *[Sara leaves in a hurry]*

Huda: Wait.... Wait.....

Narrator: Sara believes that one day someone will come and save her; so she bought the shoes to be ready for him. *[Sara appears carrying the shoes]*

Narrator: She waited and waited and waited for weeks... months... years... but... nobody came. *[Huda appears]*

Narrator: Meanwhile Huda finished her studies and had her own business. She became a successful woman.... Ten years later Sara and Huda met.

Huda: Oh! Sara!

Sara: Huda! .....How are you? I missed you!

Huda: Me too.

Sara: Oh! What a beautiful car! Who's that handsome man?

Huda: This is my car and it's my husband inside. You know... We have our own business now. What about you? Have you found your prince yet?

Sara: Not yet. I'm still waiting, but I'm sure he'll come. I think the problem is in these shoes. I must buy new ones.

Huda: Sara...stop it...You must get rid of these silly shoes and start working hard. Why should you wait for someone to save you!? Why should you wait for a superhero who may NEVER come? Sara, it's your life.... No one can save you EXCEPT YOU.

Sara: You're right Huda... You're right. *(Sara throws the shoes)*

Sara: I have many things to do.

(Huda to the audience)

Huda: What about you? You can choose to wait and wait and just wait for others to give you a happy life. And you can choose to work hard to make your happiness and determine your future. It's YOUR LIFE... It's YOUR CHOICE...

***

Abeer says...

I believe that using drama is a very effective way of teaching the English language. Students love acting and love watching drama. It helps them to learn and use authentic English. Using drama arouses their attention, emotions, motivation and helps them to have a positive attitude towards learning English. As a result, I wanted my students to write and act this play in order to share in the play writing competition held by the HUP.

I made an announcement about the competition and gave students some time to think of some ideas for the plays. Then I had a meeting with them to choose the best ideas. After that the students started writing their plays with my support, advice and recommendations . When they finished, the last step was to act and video the play. It was really a hard job but we did it successfully.

I think the students benefited greatly from this experience. They tried their hardest to write good English. They went even further than that when they lived their play by acting it. They felt every feeling and words came from their hearts rather than their mouths. No doubt that they spoke from their hearts. They were exposed to real life language. It was an unforgettable experience.

Success Story

'Success Story' was created and performed by Zaina Ahmad Hamed Mali, Khadeeja Hatem Muhammad Abu Arra, Yusra Muhammad Hafeth Abu Arra, Deema Muhammad Muheel Ghannam, and Rima' Nabeel Muhammad Abu Arra, from the Japanese Girls School, Aqqaba, Occupied Palestine, with support from their teacher, Sana' Qasrawi. A recording of the play, performed by the actors is available here ...

bit.ly/2k1fg3E

What the judges said: "A story that spans several generations all in the space of five minutes. Natural, believable acting and an uplifting ending."

Characters: **Rima'** – *a student who has a problem;* **Yusra** – *a teacher;* **Zaina** – *a doctor;* **Khadeeja** – *a teacher when she was young;* **Deema** – *Khadeeja's friend*

Rima': Teacher ... can I talk with you?

Yusra: Yes, come on. Is there any problem?!!!

Rima': ... Yesterday something happened that made me upset.

Yusra: What happened?!

Rima': While I was talking with my friends about our future and ambitions, they started laughing at me. But why? Who do they think they are?

Yusra: Oh ... Dear ... Don't worry. You are good and strong enough ... and I'm sure you will be what you hope, but you must strive to achieve your goal. Do you understand me??!!

Rima': Yes, teacher.

Yusra: And put in your mind: you must trust yourself.

Rima': We mustn't lose hope .... must we??!!

Yusra: Exactly. You know what?!! This reminds me of something. I have a diary book. I wrote about my experience. Would you like to read it??!!

Rima': Really! Can I??!! Thank you, teacher.

Rima': *[reading the diary]* When I was 15, Israeli soldiers bombed my house. My father, my mother, my dear brother were killed and my leg was injured badly. Because of that I couldn't walk again and the doctor told me ...

Zaina: This is the result of your test ..... I am sorry. You need surgery, outside the country.

Deema: Outside!!! You know it's impossible.

Zaina: Yes, I know. The Israeli occupation has prevented us from travelling outside, even for treatment.

Khadeeja: I'll never walk again.

Deema: Doctor, is surgery the only solution??!!

Zaina: No, there is physiotherapy. It is hard and it'll take a long time, but it works.

Deema: You see … you can walk again … you can ….

Khadeeja: How can I??!! Without a father … without a mother … *[starts crying]*

Deema: Don't say that, please. I'm here with you and I'm sure you can. You are very strong. Just try and I'll help you. Don't worry. …. Doctor, when can we start?

Zaina: Just a moment. I'll check the schedule.

Deema: Come on, Khadeeja …. Why are you upset? You hear, there is hope you will walk again and we're going to go shopping together. You know, I need some clothes.

Khadeeja: I don't know how to thank you. You are a really good friend.

Deema: And you are my dear friend.

Zaina: Good news. Tomorrow we can start. Be ready, Khadeeja …..

Deema: Thank you, doctor. Thank you very much. Tomorrow is the start, Khadeeja.

Rima: After 5 months of hard exercises …. I was able to walk again.

Zaina: I'm very proud of you both and I'm very happy to know such determined people like you. Congratulations to you both.

Khadeeja: Thank you, doctor. I'd never have walked again without your help; and of course Deema's help. You are so helpful.

Rima': How painful was her life! How great is my teacher .....

Rima': [in the teachers' room] Teacher, may I come in? I want to say, I'm very lucky to have such a great teacher like you.

Yusra: Oh, my dear student ... thank you. My dream was to walk again and live like others ... and you see in spite of the occupation and siege I overcame all that.... And I became a teacher. Now ... it's your turn. You mustn't give up even if you face many obstacles.

Rima': Thank you, teacher, and I promise your story will motivate me during my life.

***

Sana' says...

It was a fantastic experience to give students a space to create a story by themselves: to suggest a topic, to write out a script, to find out new vocabulary and remember old vocabulary, and to come up with an attractive title worthy of their hard work.

I, as a teacher, was very excited and happy to discover how able my students were, how great their effort could be and how creative they were.

We spent two weeks on hard training, paying great attention to pronunciation, intonation, facial expression and performance. I won't forget how enthusiastic my students were about the contest result, how much they talked about flying to London and acting out their play in a big theatre. Unfortunately, we were not the overall winners, but surely we won a lot.

The Lord of the Show

'The Lord of the Show' was created and performed by Abed Al-Rahman Mustafa Al- Najar, Ahmed Khalid Yousif, Mohammed Baha Al-Bashiti, Jana Shafiq Yousif and Sara Marwan Abed from Tel-Al sultan Elementary Co-ed UNRWA school, Gaza with the support of their teacher, Tahreer Hammad. A recording of the play, performed by the actors is available here...

bit.ly/2llAXG6

What the judges said: "An interesting and confidently delivered play about the value of team work. Quirky and highly engaging."

The Lord of the Show

Characters: **Mr. Clown; Mr. Idea; Mr. Opinion; Mr. Creativity; Mr. Conscience**

<u>Scene:</u> Mr. Idea, Mr. Creativity, Mr. Conscience, Mr. Opinion are sitting down. Mr Clown enters.

Mr. Clown: Dear ... my friend.

Mr. Creativity: Mr. Clown.

Mr. Clown: I will not be the lord of the show today. I am so sick. I am so sorry. Goodbye.

[Then they stand up and move]

Mr. Idea: Do you know me? Who am I? I am Mr. Idea. Don't worry. I will be the master of this show. No one can do anything without me. I will impress you with my magic movement. So, I must be the lord of the show.

Mr. Opinion: I am Mr. Opinion. You love me. I know that. I am your voice. You …. you and you. I decide to be or not to be. Today, I will play with my coloured balls, and all of you will clap for me. Therefore, I must be the lord of the show.

Mr. Creativity: [moves to front] I'm the lord of the show. I am Mr. Creativity. People love me. I am beauty, originality and diversity. No one has a value without me. No one can continue without me. Do you hear me? ... I am the lord of the show.

Mr. Conscience: *[moves and connects their hands together]* My dear friends, every one of you is very important. You complete each other; you give the life to the show. Every one of you is the lord of the show.

[Then they sit down. Mr. Creativity remains standing]

Mr Creativity: Look at the world with me. Come, come. See how those stars and the beautiful moon and the sun shine brightly.

The power within drives the ambition.

Know that success is on an uphill path.

The secret behind your dream.

Say ... yes. Forget the hurt and the pain

And a great rich optimism.

I lifted my head high toward the sky.

I can fulfil my dream.

and I have prepared my dream for safety.

With love I can fly to the creative world.

[They all stand up]

All: Together we can make a change.

***

Tahreer says...

This is the first time we had made a play. I tried to do something unique and new with the children. I like to discover my skills and the abilities of the kids. Some of teachers told me that there would be no benefits and the children couldn't do it. So this play was a challenge for me and to say that our young children can do it.

I read some scripts and watched some plays on Youtube. I also listened to you, Nick, when you came and told us about the plays and how to do it. Then I created an English club from third grade. I noticed that when I did group work in class, they all wanted to be a leader and there was no cooperation between them, so we had a class discussion about this problem.

The idea came from them and then I wrote the script.

The students have benefited in different ways. They like the English Language more and more. Some of students in first and second grade now want to act. It gives them the opportunity to be a leader, to have more confidence and to try something different. Their parents were so happy and they asked me to do more plays.

The prize was like a dream and the children were so happy and hopeful that they could effect a change. This experience helped me to practise writing plays. Writing and acting out a play needs training, so I hope to develop my abilities in Drama.

The Sky is your Limit

'The Sky is your Limit' was created and performed by Tala Abu Abdu, Hala Eid, Rawan Al Muhtasib, Shams Al Hams, and Malak Al Hams from Al Madina Al Monawara Prep Girls UNRWA School, Rafah with support from their teacher, Ruba El Shiqaqi. A recording of the play, performed by the actors is available here...

bit.ly/2klKUJz

What the judges said: "A passionately acted play about the inner thoughts of children living under occupation. Exciting special effects."

Characters: **Tala, Society Ghost, Self-Doubt Ghost, Angel of Positive Thinking,** *and* **Occupation Ghost.**

Tala: I wish I could ride a bike, play music, sing out loud or travel abroad.

Society Ghost: Haaa! My girl, you can't have all of these wishes.

Talal: Who are you? Why are you saying this?

Society Ghost: I'm the society you are living in. You are not allowed to achieve all of these silly dreams because you're living in this conservative society where girls can't do things against my traditions.

Tala: *[puts her hands on her head]* No, no .. I don't want to hear you. I will think of my wishes again. I want to be a successful lawyer in the future, a member in the United Nations to restore Palestinian rights.

Self-Doubt Ghost: What? What are you saying? What do you want to be?

Tala: A member in the United Nations.

Self-Doubt Ghost: Are you kidding?

Tala: No, I'm serious.

Self-Doubt Ghost: Ha ha ha ha .. I'm sorry, but you can't.

Tala: Why?

Self-Doubt Ghost: This is not easy.

Tala: I know. I will work hard.

Self-Doubt Ghost: Your abilities are not enough.

Tala: No, I'm able to do it. I'm very smart and hard-working.

Self-Doubt Ghost: Are you sure?

Tala: Yes, I'm sure. I will.

Self-Doubt Ghost: No, you can't.

Tala: No, I can.

Self-Doubt Ghost: No, you can't.

Tala: No, I can.

Angel of Positive Thinking: Keep calm, my little girl. Keep dreaming. Keep writing your wishes.

Tala: I wish I could go and see the rest of my country, Palestine. I wish I could visit Jerusalem, see the Church of Nativity, have a tour of the old city and pray in Al–Aqsa mosque.

Occupation Ghost: My charming young lady! You can't even dream of such wishes! Without our permission, you can't see your country.

Tala: Go away! Go away! I don't want to see you. I want to live in peace. I don't want to live under occupation anymore. I want to see a plane, a normal plane in our beautiful sky!

Occupation Ghost: Ha ha ha ha! Are you stupid? You can only have a nightmare of a plane dropping bombs on Gaza and nothing more.

Tala: *[puts her head on the table]*

Angel of Positive Thinking: No, no. You can't give up. You have to fight all these obstacles. Nothing can stop you. You have to fight until you reach your dreams. Stand up and start fighting.

Tala: I will keep dreaming, keep trying, and keep working. I know it's very hard, yet nothing is impossible. We, Palestinians, have the right to dream like anybody else. So, I will never say never and I will fight forever.

***

Ruba says...

This play tells the story of millions of Palestinian children living under occupation who have many dreams they wish to realize one day. It shows the obstacles they face throughout their lives and the deep belief they have in their ability to achieve their dreams. We spent days planning the performance, creating the costumes and choosing the sound and lighting effects.

The students worked as a team with all their efforts and dedication. They loved what they were doing. I still remember the passion and love I saw in their eyes while working on this play. They wanted to send a message showing the whole world that Palestinians are full of life and hope – the sky is always their limit.

This experience helped my students to discover their hidden talents and to develop not only their English language skills but also their acting, creative thinking and public speaking skills. It was really a privilege for me and my students to be part of the Hands Up playwriting competition.

Tell Me Why

'Tell me why' was created and performed by Yara Al-Najjar, Fadwa Elfar, Nagham abu Hussin and Remas Abu Amira, from Jabalia Elementary Co-ed D UNRWA school, Gaza, with support from their teacher, Ihsan Udwan. A recording of the play, performed by the actors is available here ...

bit.ly/2lBYOYj

What the judges said: "A very unique idea: explores the rights of the child in a simple but highly effective way."

Scene: *A little girl called Remas is sitting alone thinking, moonstruck. Suddenly her mind leaves her body and standing in front of her, starts talking to her.*

Little girl: Oh! I don't know what to do. I'm really bored.

Her mind: Hi, little girl. What are you doing?

Little girl: I'm doing nothing.

Her mind: All right. What about doing a new project?!

Little girl: Have you got any ideas?

Her mind: Sure, I'm thinking of Recycling Toys! It could make poor children so happy.

Little girl: Oh! Wow. That's a great idea.

[A soldier interrupts them]

Soldier: Hey! Who's this?

Little girl: It's my mind.

Soldier: What's he doing?

Little girl: He's helping me to think of new project.

Soldier: *[in an angry voice]* Who told you that you have the right to think!!??? That's not allowed.
[He takes the mind]

Scene Two: *The little girl seems to be so sad and shocked. Her heart leaves her body*

Heart: Why are you so sad little girl?

Little girl: I have just lost my right to think.

Heart: Don't be sad, dear. You still have me.

Little girl: You are right. I'll try.

Heart: You have to be strong.

[Again the soldier interrupts them with his hard voice]

Soldier: Who's this here?!

Little girl: That's my heart.

Soldier: What's he doing???

Little girl: He's helping me to feel good.

Soldier: *[in an angry voice]* Who told you that you have the right to feel!!??? That's not allowed.

[He takes the heart]

Little girl: *[in a sad voice and with tears in her eyes]* Please … wait. Tell me Why??……..

Scene Three

Soldier: What are you doing now?

Little girl: I'm doing nothing …..

Soldier: But you're existing …..

[He takes her and goes far away]

[frozen image of all the characters]

Final Scene: A very little girl called 'Hope' comes, looks surprised at their faces, then releases them.

Hope: What happened?

Soldier: What's your name??

Hope: *[in a soft voice]* My name's Hope. We have the right: to think *[releases Mind]*, to feel *[releases heart]*, to live *[releases little girl]*

Ihsan says...

The idea for Tell me Why came originally from my daughter, Yara, who liked to watch cartoons about children rights. I watched her singing in front of her friends in school. I saw the lights in Frozen cartoon and heard her friends repeat the lyrics 'tell me why' after her. That was why we decided to write a play about children rights. I helped the students with the script then gave roles to different students, testing them so as to choose the best.

My little students enjoyed themselves a lot in the rehearsals before performing the play..so many laughs, so many comic situations, so many retakes. And finally .. 'Tell me why' was born.

Who's the Master?

'Who's the Master' was created and performed by Malak Hamdan, Shatha Hamad, Sally Hweihy, Razan Hweihy and Marwa Hamad from Beit Hanoun Prep A Girls UNRWA School, Gaza with support from their teachers, Manal Ismail and Rinan AL Mazanin. A recording of the play, performed by the actors is available here ...

bit.ly/2ky9SFx

What the judges said: "A highly creative and colourful ensemble performance exploring the conflicts inside our minds."

Characters: The five human feelings: **Fear, Anger, Sadness, Disgust** *and* **Happiness.**

<u>*Scene:*</u> *A confused human head.*

[Fear appears alone]

Fear: Where has everyone gone? I can't see anyone. Oh... It's better. This place is all mine. I'll build a castle here.

[Anger appears]

Anger: Fear, hey you! Stop! How dare you? I'm here. I need a part of this place.

Fear: How?

Anger: Let's see who dominates more - *[angrily]* you or me?

Fear: You'll lose. Look around you. I spread fast. Wherever you hear bombing, airstrikes, screams, I'm here. I'm the one who makes you afraid to take crucial decisions, to face bad conditions and to plan for the unknown future. Ha ha ha!

Anger: *[speaks angrily]* That's all? Ha ha ha .... I deserve to be the master, because I'm in control nearly all the time. I'm always there when there are disturbing people, actions, assaults, injustice, brutality, violations and demonstrations. I'm like a volcano. No-one can stop me.

[Sadness appears crying. Both Fear and Anger look at Sadness]

Anger: Sadness! Oh, God!

Sadness: You forget me. What about my influence? I'm the most common feeling here. Did you forget wars, shelters, loss, homeless people, destruction, poverty and ... and ... and ... . I visit millions of peoples in a minute, break their hearts and make them sick and desperate. After that, you come to tell me you're the masters here.

[Disgust appears]

Disgust: Yuck! Hey, you shut up. Stay away from me.

Sadness: Who cares about you here, Disgust?

Disgust: But, I'm the strongest. Wherever you see rubbish, I'm there; bad smells, smoky air, I'm there. Shhhh …. Oh, listen, a disgust signal. Yes, sir. A mouldy corpse! Done.

Anger: Who you think you are?

[A quarrel breaks out between the feelings, each trying to dominate]

[Happiness appears. Seeing the quarrel, its smile fades slowly]

Fear: Oh you're always late, Happiness. Why?

Happiness: Please, stop. I'm dying. You'll kill me.

Fear: Don't do that, please. Wake up. We need you.

Disgust: That's what you all want.

Anger: You shut up! Dear Happiness, don't leave us. We need you. This place needs your laughs, smiles and your positive energy.

Happiness: In this place, I don't have much space. Whenever I appear, you kill me with your fighting and your quarrels. Oh, my heart rate is racing. I'm dying.

Sadness: Hold on, please. Hold on, we won't fight. I'm fed up. You can have my place. This world is full of sorrows, so let happiness abide here and let peace dwell here.

Disgust: Stop that confusion. It's his own decision. Happiness is a decision. If this head decides to be happy, then it will be so. Don't wait for others to make your happiness. Make it yourself.

Happiness: *[regains its strength]* You're right. Happiness can heal itself and others. Laugh the world laughs with you. Weep and you weep alone. So please, give me a chance to heal the wounds. To make it a better place, for you and for me and for the entire human race.

All feelings: Now, who's the master? The decision is yours.

***

Manal says...

Through this play, we wanted to send a massage to people all over the world, a message that says, "Happiness is a decision. Don't let bad feelings and thoughts dominate in your life. Once your brain is perplexed with terrible surroundings and black thoughts, rise up and make up your mind to choose what makes your life happier, safer and better.

We, Rinan and Manal, started asking our English club students to answer the question, "What's your concept of a human being?" Most answers contained the word "feelings", and from that sprang the idea of writing a play about a conflict of feelings in a human brain.

As you know, a human being is a mixture of feelings. Therefore, our drama club students agreed to work on the five basic feelings, which are "happiness, sadness, fear, anger and disgust". The students tried to personalize each feeling and put a spotlight on how each feeling has affected our lives.

Acting in this play, students lived an incredible experience in which every student had the chance to let her imagination go to create her own character. Shatha said, "I thought about how anger can be. I chose the red colour to symbolize anger. I learned my lesson, "Control your anger. Don't shout about trivial things. Think before you act."

Sally said, "We Palestinians are surrounded by sorrows. I wanted to tell the world that in spite of our sadness, we love life and "We Palestinians, teach life, sir", as the Palestinian poet, Rafif Zeyada, said. That's why I gave up my sadness at the end of the play and let happiness dwell everywhere. So that's it. Thanks to HUP project and Mr Great Nick our imagination can travel across borders to say, "Let love and peace abide in our country and in the whole world to enjoy a healthy human life."

Chapter 4
The Right to Development

The Right to Development seeks to guarantee that the child is given the support, care and love he or she needs to ensure optimum mental, physical and emotional development. Mental development comes through education, physical development through play and adequate nutrition and emotional development through a network of family and community. **I Will Wait Till They Open the Gate** uses strong symbolism to show how these conditions for development are greatly restricted for Palestinians. **Future Gates** and **Ambition Play** send strong messages about the value of education, while **Don't Stop** and **Be What You Want focus on** the importance of parental support in allowing children to develop as they want. In **Othman the Honest**, the children use a parable to highlight the importance of honesty with one's community. Finally, **The Play of the Play** uses the play competition itself as its subject matter, highlighting the opportunities it could bring.

I will wait until they open the gate

'I will wait until they open the gate' was created and performed by Sara, Afaf, Abeer, Reema and Saja from Beach Elem Co-ed School (C), Gaza with support from their teacher, Luzan Matar. A recording of the play, performed by the actors is available here ...

bit.ly/2koqtM8

What the judges said: "Portrays the frustrations, determination and resilience of children living under a blockade. Hauntingly moving."

Scene: *A group of animals are waiting behind a wide closed gate. They are whispering with unintelligible words; each one has its own story. A monkey sees the animals who are waiting near the gate. He wonders why they are waiting and starts to ask each of them to find out the reason.*

Monkey: Good morning, sir. What happened to you? Why are you waiting here?

Elephant: Hello dear. Why are you asking? I've been waiting here for a long time. I am waiting for my freedom, but there is no response. No-one believes me that I want to live a peaceful life without fear. I want to go everywhere without any borders or limits.

Monkey: But who prevents you?

Elephant: This awful gate. You don't know what this gate means to us! Anyway, I will wait here till they open the gate.

Monkey: But who are they? What do you mean?

[The Elephant keeps silent and the monkey repeats the questions several times till the monkey hears a little baby rabbit and his mother. They are crying and his mother is trying to calm him down]

Monkey: Hello, Mrs. Rabbit. What happened to you and your baby?

Mrs. Rabbit: *[while she is crying]* Look at my baby. The baby is hungry and I have nothing to feed him. I don't know what to do for him. What did my little baby do to them? I will wait till they open the gate.

Monkey: Who are they? What do you mean?

[Mrs. Rabbit keeps silent with no response. The monkey sees a sad giraffe holding a book]

Monkey: Why are you sad, Mr. Giraffe? What happened to you? Why are you holding this book?

Mr. Giraffe: I want to learn.

Monkey: Really. Ha ha ha. What do you want to learn? Is it important for you?

Mr. Giraffe: Of course, who do you think you are? Why are you laughing? I have the right to learn like anyone in the world. It is important. Learning will pave the way for me for this wide world.

Monkey: *[still laughing]* But why can't you learn?

Mr. Giraffe: Can't you see this gate! It is our big problem, our big challenge. Shame on you! I will wait till they open the gate.

Monkey: *[repeats the same questions]* Who are they? What do you mean?

[The monkey stops laughing and looks around. He finds a weak and tired horse and speaks to him]

Monkey: What happened to you?

Horse: I am very tired and thirsty. I don't feel OK. It looks like I'm ill, but I don't have any medicine.

[The monkey tries to help the horse, but it is too late, the horse is very weak]

Monkey: Oh, poor horse, hold on please. Don't worry. I am going to ask for help for you.

The horse: *[in a low and weak voice]* We have waited here for a long time, but with no response. Maybe someone one day will come and open the gate so we can have freedom, food, water, knowledge, and medicine. We may have our right to live, to live as others live. I will wait here till they open the gate.

[All the animals stand together, walk towards the gate, and repeat]

All: We will wait till they open the gate.

***

Luzan says...

We wrote this play for two reasons. The first was to tell people that Palestinians are kind; their only wish is to live peacefully. They suffer and live under tough circumstances, but they believe that one day all of their problems will be solved. We wanted to convey a message to everyone in the world that Palestinian children deserve a decent life like other children around the world. The second reason was to create and build the students' characters so that they would be able to stand in front of an audience, using English confidently and fluently to express their feelings and emotions. They can tell others who they are and share with others their ideas and problems.

The play involved cooperation between me and my students. I am a good friend to all my students and I usually listen to them and their problems. Their sufferings were the inspiration for this play, but it was a challenge to get these ideas into a five minute play at the students' English level.

This experience will never be forgotten. It was the students' opportunity to travel to the West Bank for the first time. They are brave and they can use English more fluently and confidently.

Othman the Honest

'Othman the Honest' was created and performed by Omar Al Farra, Mo'ataz Abu Dahwod, Khalil Abu Shennar, Karam Lehjouj and Mahmoud Dohan from Khan Younis Prep Boys school, Gaza, with support from their teacher, Rami M. Abu Hatab. A recording of the play, performed by the actors is available here ...

bit.ly/2lYMwsX

What the judges said: "A wonderful parable play about the value of honesty with an unexpected twist at the end. Visually very attractive."

Scene: *A narrator stands centre stage; in the background we can see a royal palace*

Narrator: Once upon a time there was a good and fair king. He loved his people so much, but he loved nature above all else. He spent many hours caring for the thousands of flowers in his garden.

Scene One

The Servant: You look tired, my Sire. You look tired.

The King: Yes, my son. And I am getting older. Listen, my son. I am afraid for my people's future. So I need a good person to be the new king and to look after these people.

The Servant: So, what should you do, Sire?

The King: Look! I have an idea.

The Servant: What is it, Sire? What is it?

The King: Listen carefully! I want you to call all the children in my kingdom.

The Servant: OK, Sire. OK.

Scene Two

The Servant: All the children in the kingdom, come to the palace, please. All the children in the kingdom, come to the palace, please.

The King: You are welcome, my little sons. You are welcome.

The King: Listen, everybody! I will give each of you a seed and I want you to plant it in a pot and return with a flower in a year.

The Children: OK, Sire. OK.

The King: Now, go and look after your seeds carefully. Go.

Scene Three

[Two months later. Othman appears on the stage caring for his seed very well, talking to himself]

Othman: I planted my seed and looked after it carefully, but it didn't grow. What happened? What's wrong? I don't know.....

[One year later]

Narrator: The end of the year arrived and Othman still had an empty pot.

Scene Four

[All the children appear on the stage holding their pots with beautiful flowers except Othman who has an empty pot. Then the King appears]

The King: You. Come here, please. What's your name?

Othman: My name is Othman.

The King: What happened to your seed, my son?

Othman: I watered my seed carefully, but it didn't grow, my Sire. I am so sorry.

I am so sorry.

[The other children laugh loudly]

The King: [shouting angrily] Keep silent! I don't know what you have been growing. I gave you cooked seeds which don't grow. Othman is the only honest child in my kingdom, and he shall be the next king.

***

Rami says...

The idea for our play started when you (the Hands Up Project) announced the competition. When we knew that there was a competition, we decided to participate in it full of energy and enthusiasm.

The idea for the play came from one of the famous stories found in English for Palestine „Grade 7 book „, the old version. The students had already learned this story and we decided to make it into a play.

When we had found the right students to act out the story, I started to coach them after the school day with help from my colleagues. When the students were ready, I asked some local associations and volunteers to provide us with the necessary equipment to video the play and when everything was ready, we videoed the play and sent it.

Luckily, we were one of the winners!!!

It was a great experience from which I really benefitted on a personal level and from which the students who participated also benefitted greatly. I noticed that their language started to improve over time and through the training. Also, they learned many new skills in acting and drama. I'd like to thank Mr. Nick for giving us the chance to participate in this great competition.

Future Gates

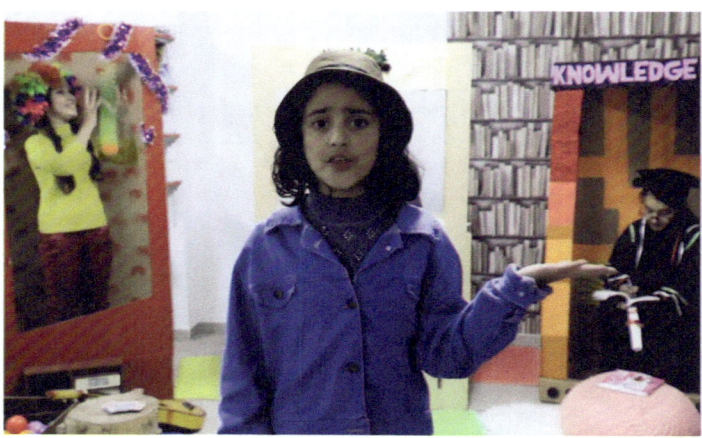

'Future Gates' was created and performed by Sara Deva, Aya Hakam, Noor Basem, and Layan Ahmed from Faqua Girls' Secondary School, Jenin, Palestine with support from their teacher, Abeer Adel Alrahman Isleem. A recording of the play, performed by the actors is available here ...

bit.ly/2kxWOjv

What the judges said: "An original and life affirming message about the value of education and knowledge delivered with conviction. Great props and scenery."

Scene One: *A student, Reda, is very confused whether to complete his difficult studies or not. He is looking around in a lost way. There are three doors.*

Reda: I've finished my secondary education and I'm confused whether to complete higher education or to choose another way. All these doors around me, so where should I go? I'll try this one.

[He opens the door and hears loud music. Then he stands behind the door]

Door 1: I'm the world of business .You don't have to study .Go straight to work .You don't have to waste your time with boring learning. Exploit your chance of having great wealth and huge fame.

You will be very rich in a very short period, whereas your friends will be still struggling at university. Then what? Do you know? Can you guess? You will sign a formal financial transaction which will take your wealth away due to your ignorance in both accountancy and other types of sciences. Your stupidity will lead you to lose everything you have gained, even a bit of food. Ha ha ha ha ha ha!

Reda: No, no. Not this way. I'm going to try the other.

[He goes out fearfully, wearing a torn cloak]

[He opens the door. He hears loud music and noise. He stands behind the door and it speaks]

Door 2: I'm the door of bad friends, enjoying wasting time, smoking, gambling, and using the internet a lot. Here you won't work; you won't study. You'll be ignorant, poor, and have a very bad future and may end up in a prison. Ha ha ha ha ha ha!

[He rapidly goes out, tired and coughing, to the next door]

Reda: Oh, oh my god. Not this way *[taking the cloak off]* It's my last destination. What could it be? *[He opens the door and hears calm music]*

Door 3: I'm the knowledge world. You can access this place in several ways. I'm the brightness path. On this road you can find the answers for every question. You can also have the best solution for your problems. Here you will work hard at the beginning and earn much at the end. Here you will achieve your childhood dreams to be an advocate to defend your dignity and the issue of your Palestinian homeland. Here you will learn Arabic, English, French, and so many different languages. Here, dreams will come true.

[Reda goes out wearing graduation clothes holding a certificate and two candles. She gives one to the first door]

Reda: Learning is the flame for your darkness.

[She gives the other candle to the other door]

Reda: Learning is the light for your work.

All: The pen is mightier than the sword.

***

Abeer says...

The idea for our play developed from the belief that each of us aspires to a bright future which can often be reached through education.

We noticed as teachers that drama has a great effect on Palestinians students who live under an Israeli occupation which tries to destroy their dreams. It's better for those students to discover the impact of education through this attractive medium of a play.

There is no better time to begin thinking about the importance of education than the early teen years; to recognise education as the gateway to attaining dreams and countless wishes. Then they will consider it as a sword to fight their real enemies.

Don't Stop

'Don't stop' was created and performed by Malak Ahmad Al Batniji, Nagham Nabil Hijaz, Shahed Raaed Al Wehadi, Dima Anwar Awad Allah, and Zina Ahmad Zaqout from Mamounia Prep A UNRWA school, Gaza, with the support of their teacher, Shereen Hamed Lubbad. A recording of the play, performed by the actors is available here ...

bit.ly/2lK6B64

What the judges said: "A well-implemented play tackling the harrowing issue of child marriage in a playful and poignant manner."

Narrator : Dana was thirteen years old. She was hopping in an open area. Her mother came happily with "good news".

Dana: Hop, hop,

Don't stop.

I will play.

I will grow.

I will be a mother too.

Her mother: Congratulations, honey. You are a bride. Congratulations!

[The lights of the wedding's party are turned on and the flowers are spread]

Dana: I am a bride! With a crown. I am a princess!

Narrator: Two years later, Dana appeared in a miserable condition, carrying a baby. She started hopping while she was crying and singing.

Dana: Hop, hop,

Don't stop.

I am young.

I am a mother.

I'm also divorced.

[Dana's father encourages her, giving her some books and a school uniform]

Narrator: Dana's father felt sorry. He spoke to her sadly ...

Dana's Father: I am sorry. Don't worry, my darling. I will never let you down again. I will support you. Go back to your school and start a new life.

Dana: Start a new life! Are you serious, Dad? Oh! Thank God. I am so happy.

Narrator: Dana was carrying books. She started reading.

Dana: Back to school! I am a student in Al Mamounia Prep School (A).

Narrator: And a little girl came hopping and singing.

The girl: Hop, hop,

Don't stop.

I will play.

I will grow.

I will be a mother too.

Dana: Stop. Don't be in a hurry, dear. Trust me. The white dress is a trap. Give me your hand. Let's hop.

[they hop together]

Hop, hop, don't stop. I will read. I will know. Until I've studied, I'll say NO, NO, NO.

[Dana gives the little girl a book]

Dana: Enjoy your childhood.

Team: Take your time to grow. Life is so sweet. Read, learn, and enjoy.

***

Shereen says... We made this play to talk about a burning issue in Palestinian society of early marriage. In this play, we represented the bad impact of early marriage (divorce and having a baby). We used the hopping game to show the different stages of the hero's life. We wanted to send a message to parents to stop early marriage and to give a chance to their daughters to live their childhood and to complete their education. Also, another message is that life will not stop: you can complete your life, education and get rid of all of the obstacles that you face in your life. For that reason we called the play 'Don't Stop'.

We made the play with the help of one of the student's parents, Mrs Samaher Al Kuzendar. She helped and shared ideas about the play.

My students enjoyed the experience of acting and sending a real message about early marriage .Also, they enjoyed developing their English language and they hope to participate again in the Hands Up Project.

Be What You Want

'Be What You Want' was created and performed by Baha'aldin Jihad Abo Hmaid, Hikmat Ali Hmaidat, Tarneem Ibrahim Abo Hmaid, Ibrahim Ali Dawood, and Balqis Jabr Hmaidat from Om Lasafa Basic school, Hebron, Palestine with support from their teacher Ayman Hroosh. A recording of the play, performed by the actors is available here ...

bit.ly/2k5WisR

What the judges said: "A dramatic play about family roles - well-produced and acted with skill and enthusiasm. You can sense the family closeness."

Characters: **Mum, Dad, Marwa** *(their daughter),* **Amal** *(Marwa's sister),* **Rami** *(Marwa's disabled brother)*

Narrator 1: Learning things is important for life.

Narrator 2: But everyone has to learn something useful.

Narrator 1: Marwa is very happy. She did very well in Al-Injaz exam. She wants to study English.

Narrator 2: Marwa's dad thinks that a doctor is better than a teacher. He wants to plan his children's future.

Marwa: Dad, Dad. I've got 95 in Al-Injaz exam, I'm so happy. I did it.

Dad: Oh yes, you're a good girl, honey. You'll be a great doctor. My daughter is a doctor.

Marwa: Doctor!?

Dad: Yes, I always dream of this moment, and you will do it.

Marwa: Sorry, Dad, but my dream's to be an English teacher.

Dad: What!?? W-w-w-w-what's that? What did you say? A teacher!? No, no, no. Never. A-a-a-a-are you going to kill me? You.....

Marwa: Please dad no, I love you so much. But I've never thought about being a doctor. You are my dad, and you have to support me. You ......

Narrator 2: Dad is getting angry and his voice gets louder and louder.

Dad: *[shouting at her]* Stop it, Marwa!!

Narrator 1: Marwa's struggling with her dad's decision, but with just one tool: hope.

Narrator 2: Dad has lost his mind and Marwa's crying when Mum knocks on the door.

Mum: Aah, oh no, no ... Sweetheart, why are you crying? What's going on?

Narrator 2: Marwa's hugging her mum like a young bird that fell from the nest with no hope of keeping alive. And in the blink of an eye she flies again on her mum's wings.

Mum: Don't cry honey, you're great. You've got 95. Why are you crying? You must be happy. We're proud of you.

Dad: Accidents will happen!

Mum: What do you mean dear?

Dad: I'm so exhausted, I devoted all my life to you. And now she wants to be a teacher. Why? Why?

Marwa: Yes, I want to be a teacher, this is what I want to be. Please mum, tell him that. Please, please.

Mum: Oh honey, calm down, calm down. You will. [to her husband] Look dear, you can't do things in this way. She has to decide her future from this moment. We have to support her.

Dad: Nonsense! She has to be a doctor.

Amal: Dad, please. Marwa always tells me she wants to be a teacher. And I want to be a nurse. So, next year you will do the same to me!? Won't you?

Dad: Yes, you will be what I want. You are young; you don't understand life. You have to be old enough to do this.

Mum: After we had married, you forbade me to complete my education. I didn't care then. I said, we'll have a happy family, and my children will be great, and now you're doing the same to them. Why? Why are you doing this?

Narrator 1: Mum's crying, but she knows that she has to be strong enough to help her children.

Narrator 2: Dad listens to his wife and he is affected by her words.

Mum: Look, I'll never let you destroy my children. I didn't care about myself, but don't do that to my children. You have to help them. You have to make them happy, not cry.

Rami: Y-y-y-y-y-yes Dad, y-y-y-y-y-you have t-t-t-to h-h-help us, m-m-m-mum's r-right, I'll be a pianist. I l-l-l-love p-p-p-p-playing the p-p-piano. P-p-please, Daaaaad, p-p-please.

Dad: When I was a boy, I dreamed of being a pilot. Huhhh. Yes, but my dad died that year. So I had to work day and night to feed my young sisters. Then I lost my dream. You know, children, I love you and I care for you. I'm sorry, my children, I'm sorry. I will not kill your dreams. Be what you want, and I'm sure, I'll be proud of you.

Family: *[together]* Don't be your children. Let them be what they want. Let them fly.

***

Ayman says...

In our community most parents force their children to do things they don't necessarily want to do. From here the idea of our play was born. My students loved the idea because it touches their own lives. We have to give our children many choices to let them fly into their future happily. Sometimes no one can understand your deeper feelings, not even your parents. So, it's important to hold onto your dream, because you will not find another."Be What You Want".

Ambition play

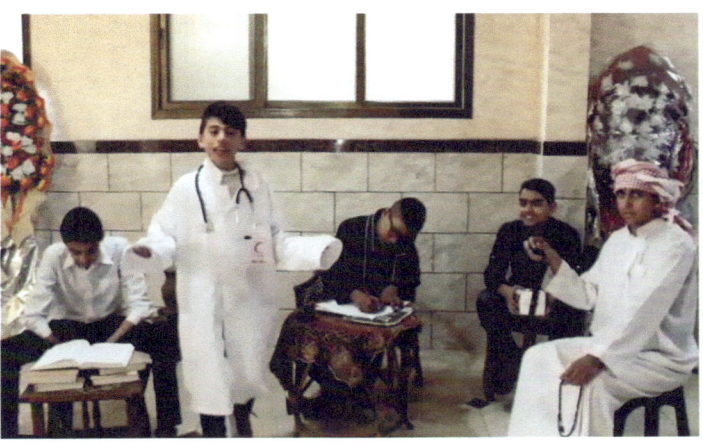

'Ambition play' was created and performed by Ibraheem Nabil Qoud, Kamal Rami Abdel-Al, Jameel Hilmi Abu Dalal, Abdel Haleem Imad Abu Shawiesh, Ahmad Mohammad Abu Shawiesh from Nusierat Prep 'D' Boys' (UNRWA) School, Gaza, with support from their teacher, Husam Mohammad Matar. A recording of the play, performed by the actors is available here …

bit.ly/2m6LJqd

What the judges said: "A well-acted play about how to reach your goals combining dialogue with direct addressing of the audience. Great theme for young people. "

Ambition play

Characters: **Dad, Book, Close friend, Teacher, Ahmad** *(future doctor)*

<u>Scene:</u> *Five students gather in a western corner to perform this play. Dad sits on the right. A friend sits next to him. A teacher sits in the middle and the book sits on the left. They all look east to face the camera. Ahmad (future doctor) enters from the south.*

[Ahmad enters wearing a doctor's coat and holding a stethoscope. He looks at the audience and goes to the book, the teacher, the friend, and the dad in turn. All of them look wonderingly!!]

Dad: What's that?!!

Friend: Are you a crazy boy?! You look funny!!

Teacher: Who's that?!

Book: (addresses friend): it's so funny!

Friend: You are right.

Ahmad: *[moves forward and addresses the audience]* Why do you look at me like this? I know you're all wondering how come a little boy is wearing a doctor's coat! But this is my dream and I will tell you what makes me sure to be a doctor.

Others: *[shout amazed]* Doctor!!!

Ahmad: *[looks back and replies smilingly]* Yes, a doctor..

Ahmad: *[addresses the audience trustingly]* Come with me and I will tell you the secret *[lowers his voice]* Just come, don't worry.. *[he goes back to his Dad]*

Ahmad: From here my success will begin.

[Dad stands with a stick in his hand. He catches Ahmad's hand and addresses the audience]

Dad: In our religion you are all shepherds and all of you are responsible for his flock. We are responsible for our sons. That's why we should care a lot about all the details of their life and help them to make their dreams come true.

[Dad then addresses Ahmad]

Dad: I'm very proud of you my son.

Ahmad: Thank you, Dad *[kisses dad's hand]*

Dad: God bless you. *[Dad sits down]*

[Ahmad looks at the audience and moves to the teacher]

Ahmad: Stand up for the teacher and respect him. He could have been a messenger.

Teacher: *[addresses the audience]* Our students are like a plant. We must water and feed them with knowledge and science to grow and to become useful.

Teacher: *[to Ahmad]* Go on, my best student. I'm sure you will reach your noble goal.

Ahmad: Thank you, my teacher .

[Ahmad moves to the book]

Ahmad: A book holds a house of gold.

The book: *[to audience]* I'm good for the brain and the soul and you have always been with me, getting information. So take anything from me and successfully have whatever you can.

The book: *[addresses Ahmad]* We hope you reach your dream.

Ahmad: Thank you, my book.

[Ahmad walks forward and addresses the audience]

Ahmad: A person is likely to follow the habits of his friend so be aware of whom you take as a friend. *[Ahmad points to his friend. The friend stands up and goes to Ahmad and addresses him]*

Friend: You look great in this uniform.

Ahmad: Yes...

Friend: But I think it is something funny to wear a doctor's coat.

Ahmad: OK.

Friend: Yes. Listen. I will tell you this advice, so take it..

Ahmad : OK..

Friend: When you choose a friend, you should choose one who looks like you in everything and with him you can achieve all your dreams and reach success.

[Ahmad catches his friend's hand]

Ahmad: Thank you, my friend. *[The friend goes back to his seat]*.

Ahmad: *[addresses the audience]* When the basis is solid and all success factors are available to you, it's very easy to achieve your dream and be whatever you want…

Friend: *[on his way to Ahmad, completes his sentence]* …. and as you see, when someone supports you and you work hard, you will be a doctor… Oh, I mean whatever you dream.. … And now I'll tell you all the success factors: first, the Dad *[points to Dad]*

[Dad stands up and joins Ahmad and friend]

Dad: *[to Ahmad]* Well done, Ahmad.. keep going and you will be a doctor.

Ahmad and friend: *[appreciatively]* Thanks to Dad.

Friend: ….second, the book … *[points to the book]*

[The book goes over to Ahmad and supports him]

Book: *[to Ahmad]* We hope to fulfil your dream.

Friend: … third, the teacher…

[The teacher joins the group]

Teacher: *[to Ahmad and the audience]* My student.. I'm sure you will reach your noble goal. And you *[points to the audience]* can reach your noble goal.

[Finally, all the actors hold each other's' hands and bow to the audience respectfully]

***

Husam says...

First of all I want to thank the Hands Up Project team for allowing us to participate in this activity. In fact, it was an interesting experience that all of us benefited from. The work began after I had read the conditions of the competition. I told the students of 8th and 9th grades about it. A lot of students were enthusiastic about the idea and from these I chose four talented students to discuss the idea and take it forward. They came up with many ideas. Finally, we agreed on a play about ambition and how human beings can reach it. The students knew their roles and tested out their lines until they mastered the performance. I'd like to say that this experience was very fruitful. The students benefited a lot from it. They practised their second language very well and they also learned about drama and how they could use it to send constructive messages. Moreover, the students were very pleased and they insisted on participating in other similar activities in future.

The Play of the Play

'The Play of the Play' was created and performed by Lama Abu Shqeer, Zena Al Masri, Elham Ashour, Lina Al Jbour and Noor Al Shamaly from Al Fukhari Prep. Girls UNRWA School, Khan Younis, Gaza with support from their teacher, Inas Younis Shurrab. A recording of the play, performed by the actors is available here…

bit.ly/2k5HVVj

What the judges said: "A creative, witty and convention-breaking play whose subject is the play competition itself. Full of energy and joy."

Scene One: Lama is sitting on her desk, watching a video on her mobile phone. We hear the voice of Mr. Nick, talking about the Hands up project "The Palestinian children are, in my experience, the most creative, the most engaging, the most motivated children that I've ever worked with anywhere in the world ."

Lama: *[proudly]* Yes, Mr. Nick, you are right. We are the most creative children in the world and I will work very hard to prove your words. I will show my creativity to you and to the whole world.

Zena: *[holding a toy in her hands]* What are you doing, Lama? Come and play with me.

Lama: I can't play now Zena. I'm busy. I'm writing a story in English……. I'll write about you and me. Can you help me, Zena?

Zena: *[thinking]* You can write about what happened yesterday … *[flying the toy in her hand]* Remember? Zzzzzzzzzzzz….bomb. [sadly] I was very scared, Lama. I couldn't even sleep. And look at my bear. He said that we couldn't go out to play in the garden. It's dangerous.

Lama: Yes, dear. You're right. I will write about those tears in your eyes and those toys in your hands; about the hope in your heart .. Zena, what do you hope to be?

Zena: Yes, I hope to be a doctor to treat my friend, Maha. She is very ill and when I grow up, I will be a doctor and give her the medicine.

Lama: *[singing]* When you grow big and tall, big and tall, big and tall ..What do you want to be?

[Zena sings with her]

Zena and Lama: I want to be a doctor, I want to be a doctor, I want to be a doctor. Let me check your temperature. *[they laugh]*

[Lama picks her pencil and starts to write]

Mother: *[coming into Lama's room]* What are you doing, Lama? What are you writing, dear?

Lama: Oh, mum. The English teacher told us to write a story of a play about our life. And I told Zena that I will write about me and her.

Zena: And our toys …

Lama: *[smiling]* Yes, and the toys.

Lama: *[whispering]* Mother, I will show you my play when I finish .. If we win, many people will see our play and we may travel.

Mother: *[whispering]* Where ?

Lama: *[whispering]* To London.

Mother: *[shouting]* To London .. Are you serious?

[Lama nods her head and smiles]

Mother: Inshallah, you will win. I will pray for you .. Lama, are you going to take us with you?

Lama: *[laughing]* OK, mum. OK.

Narrator: The next day, Lama went to her teacher to show her the play. The teacher read the play and she was very pleased with Lama.

<u>*Scene Two:*</u> *Lama is standing with her teacher.*

The teacher: Excellent, Lama. I will see you in the break to write our final script.

<u>*Scene Three:*</u> *The teacher is putting her arms behind Lama's shoulders and they are walking and talking, but we can't hear what they are saying.*

Narrator: The next day, Lama started her training for the play with the help of her teacher. She was very motivated and they worked hard to do their best.

Teacher: *[wondering]* What should we call it?

Lama: *[thinking]* What about "the play"?

Teacher: *[slowly]* Wonderful. The play of the play.

[Two cards appear: "A week later" and 'The Play of the Play' won first place". A voice of the winning sound effect .. "TaDa"]

Scene Four: *The teacher is calling Lama*

Teacher: *[happily]* Lama, our play won the first place. Alhamdilullah. We won, we won.

Lama: *[happily]* Thank Allah that we won. Yes, we did it. We did it.

[Zena and her mother appear suddenly and the mother is talking to Lama]

Mother: Lama, what about your promise?

Teacher: *[wondering]* What's going on Lama ? What was your promise?

Lama: I promised my mum and Zena I'd take them with me to London.

Teacher: *[laughing]* Of course, we will. Because you are two characters in our play.

[Everyone laughs. Lama and Zena sing their song – 'When you grow big and tall']

***

Inas says...

When I heard of the Hands Up project remote theatre competition, I was so excited to join and try to win. I decided to put to use all the experience I had gained during the summer training course by sharing it with my colleagues and students. Therefore, I started up a drama club at my school. After some meetings, I told my students that we had to start making our own play for the competition. Actually, I used the motivation of persuading them how beautiful it will be to participate and win. Some of them brought some nice stories about different topics and they were very enthusiastic. I realised how this would help them to improve all of their English skills.

We tried to make our play as unique as possible. Therefore, we decided to talk about our own experience with the competition .We agreed on the characters and the script. When I finished the first edition, I sent the file to my supervisor, Mr. Mohamad Al Astal who suggested some changes, namely talking more about the life of children in Gaza and that was Zena's role which added a great message to the play.